I0411724

FOREST SERVICE LOST

A look back at the National Forest and the Agency
that manages these Forests
A look forward to a proper direction and support for
the Agency

GEOFFREY W HARVEY

Copyright © 2015 Geoffrey W Harvey

ISBN-13:978-1511751308

ISBN-10: 1511751304

DEDICATION

This comment of on status of our peoples' national forests, the agency entrusted with their management and the remedies possible is dedicated to the hearty souls knowing these lands, who have been and remain willing to join the often fierce battle to protect and preserve these very special lands. The work is dedicated to all who would strive to maintain and fully realize Theodore Roosevelt's vision of national forests and legacy of balanced management for all the resources of these lands.

CONTENTS

Prologue

During the mid-1960s Ranger Roan Andersen was the guiding hand, face, and boss of the Roosevelt National Forest's Redfeather Ranger District. Even then, nearly fifty years ago, the budget had been cut from those of the agency's heyday in the 1930s, primarily to help support a foreign war. Roan had a minimal permanent staff consisting of an Assistant District Ranger, General District Assistant, and a secretary-dispatcher. The summer crew included the veteran fire lookout up on the Deadman Tower and seven college students young and old. All the summer crew was spending the summer working for the U. S. Forest Service to gain some practical experience in forest management at the bottom rung of the ladder and also to pick up some spending money. The money would soon be spent chasing the girls in nearby Estes Park or buying the newest of alpine skis in anticipation of the winter to follow. The experience would last a lifetime in their memory and allow these fledgling foresters to assess whether Roan's life was what they wanted their lives to be someday.

In those pre-National Forest Management Act days of the 1960s no one could envision the dramatic changes the Forest Service would undergo and continue to undergo in the latter half of the twentieth and first decade of the twenty-first century. These were the last golden days when timber cuts went largely unopposed, Lassie was the agency's propaganda front piece, and the first wilderness areas were declared. These first wildernesses included the Rawah of the Medicine Bow Range, which was easily viewed from the Deadman Tower. These were the last days of the great old time rangers like Roan who prowled their districts by truck and horse. These rangers were primarily concerned with the work being completed in their districts rather than planning and paperwork. These were the days when the agency still carried a pride of itself and its mission right out on its lapel with the badge. This was a pride instilled by Teddy Roosevelt and Gifford Pinchot and nurtured over the years by the rangers dedicated to their districts and the forest and range lands entrusted to them. These were not better times, just more innocent times when there was still plenty of forest lands across the west, still few claims on the forests as compared to today's claims by many multifaceted interest groups, and still plenty of room for land management errors to be lost in the larger landscape-both geographic and political.

Roan Andersen may have been the last of the early breed of forest rangers, in the tradition of Joe Halm and Ed Pulaski. These men were molded in part by strict parameters created by Gifford Pinchot, but also molded by the size of the domain they managed and the sheer energy required to oversee such large areas with the far less sophisticated equipment and vehicles than are available today. These men were sculpted by the harsh realities of rural western life.

Roan was a tall man, made more substantial by middle age. His strawberry blond hair hid the graying well that must have been creeping in. Assessing that feature of the man was difficult since Roan was seldom spotted without headgear of some type. Out in the field where the crews saw him almost exclusively, he was topped by a cowboy hat with a prominent sweat stain along the band above the brim. This type of hat seemed to be top Forest Service personnel's guard against any danger from above, whether sunshine or falling tree. Although the crews routinely wore hardhats as prescribed in the District's requisite safety plan, Roan was never spotted using one. Roan wore the dress uniform of a forest ranger exclusively when on the job. His wife or close friends likely saw him in different clothing. The crews saw him in the dark Forest Service green pants, a tan long sleeved shirt with the brass U. S. Forest Service badge affixed near a breast pocket, a string tie and the green Forest Service jacket, emblem stenciled at the breast, occasionally zipped closed, but typically open. His footgear was invariably cowboy boots. Even on an occasion when visited at the winter office in Fort Collins, Roan wore the uniform of his station, District Forest Ranger, only with the jacket replaced by a blazer.

When out on the district, Roan drove the standard light green Dodge truck that was nearly emblematic of the agency in those years. The Forest Service shield was decaled on the two doors. The truck pulled a tan, brown, and rust one-horse trailer nearly all the time. From the perspective of the crews, Roan went no place without his horse in tow. The crews most often saw Roan pull up to the project on which they were working, if it could be reached by road. After a few words with Bill Hurd, the General District Assistant, he would fetch his tall chestnut horse from the back of the trailer. The saddle blanket followed by the saddle and then the reigning gear were placed in rapid fashion. Roan would mount up and ride off for a more extensive examination of the work completed. If a crew was working trails or bark beetle control well down the trail from the trailhead or at some remote location, Roan was sure to appear atop his horse to have a firsthand look at your work. He would have a few words with the crew, make suggestions if he felt it necessary to do so and then move on to other oversight tasks. His instructions and knowledge of the work at hand left the crewman little doubt that he had operated a spray can, brushing axe or chainsaw more than enough to know all the tricks you were yet to learn. From the perspective of the seasonal college hire, Roan Andersen, the ranger and boss, was also in large part, an ephemeral ghost that appeared for a short time,

4

viewed the scene, possibly offered some suggestions and as rapidly disappeared off into the woods, typically in the opposite direction from which he came. The crewmen had little time to understand or contemplate Roan's schedule, but did wonder aloud from time to time whether most of his day was just a pleasant ride in the forest.

Roan must have spent more than his share of time out on the district lands. There was little other explanation of his thorough and intimate knowledge of its terrain and resources. During this author's brief mid-1960s tenure on the Redfeather District, the checkerboard lands owned alternately by the railroad and federal government located but a few miles north of the village of Redfeather Lakes and stretching north to and beyond the Wyoming border, were a no man's land that the district crews entered once during his time and then only to put out a lightning strike fire. The fire fight was confined largely to the dusk and night hours, so we saw little and learned less about the surrounding countryside. During that summer this author was especially intrigued by that country, because Black Mountain that stood up in its midst was legend as the location of a lost gold strike. Try as I would at that time to find an approach to this landmark, no clear road or trail was found. Yet Roan spoke of being there and elsewhere all across the mysterious north end of the district. From his understated and matter of fact description of the area, he had covered most of it from the jumbled rock piles of the "gang plank" county to the east along the front range, west to the lodgepole and spruce forests covering the slopes of the Baldys and Deadman Mountain, from the hot dry south facing slopes of the Poudre Canyon to the Wyoming line. Roan knew his district as well and maybe better than Bill Hurd his General District Assistant who grew up in and ranched most of his adult life in the Redfeather Lakes Country.

Roan possessed all the characteristics of dress, equipment and knowledge of the old time forest rangers. His job was to manage the district which translated to him to hands on management of the land and its resources as a direct supervisor. Even then he was buffeted by political pressure from higher ups in the Denver Supervisors Office and further up the political hierarchy to get out more timber cut. He resisted political manipulation with some but not complete success. He was a man who knew his district its resources and needs. He managed with but a small modicum of scientific foundation and technical input most of which was supplied by "experts" from the Supervisor's Office. He conserved the forest and protected it from harm as it was perceived in his day.

Roan Andersen and rangers like him moved off into retirement in the early 1970s. They were replaced with rangers as well-meaning but far less connected to the land they managed. During the mid to late 1960s a social change had occurred on the districts of the Forest Service. Before that time rangers and their families lived at the district headquarters either year around, if a town was not close enough at hand, or at least during the summer months. The initial task of most summer crews, ours included, was to fill the copious basement of the ranger's residence with firewood. The wood supply saw the ranger and his family through the next winter season when the crews were gone. By the 1960s pressure from their life partners and the advent of more reliable and comfortable trucks made it possible for more rangers to live in nearby towns and commute to work on the district on a daily basis. Just prior to leaving the area word was received that Roan too had compromised with his spouse and set up shop in Fort Collins on a permanent basis. This was an initial step in a progression of district and forest amalgamations and management of those amalgamated forest lands from more distant offices. A short decade and a half later as the forest planning process mandated by the National Forest Management Act was in full swing, it became obvious to participants who knew the landscape that the forest managers writing the plans had a far hazier notion of the landscape and its resources that was often gleaned from maps rather than from the experience of covering the ground and knowing the resources it possessed.

Roan Andersen and rangers like him became an extinct commodity in the Forest Service after 1980. The cumulative sins of overcutting the national forest and the resulting large clear-cuts which were largely driven by political pressures to get out the cut resulted in the environmental backlash that brought forward the National Forest Management Act. The Act was to give all users a say in the management of the national forests. A casualty of this process was the old time rangers. A new breed of rangers and technocrats stepped into the line leadership. These were the political front men who took Lassie's place when she was placed on the junk heap of worn out propaganda tools. These rangers transferred in for roughly four year stints. They were happy to know their districts from the road, an airplane or maps, but prefer the safe confines of the office advised by technical experts often less willing to know first-hand the resources they made decisions concerning.

One low point may have been reached in the 1980s. During a meeting on the initial Flathead Forest Plan, the bright young expert forest planner who would later rise within a decade and a half to the highest position in the Forest Service, required correction by a member of the public on his calculation of riparian forest acres.

The participant pointed out that the calculation was off to the low side by a factor of two. The planners had failed to allow in their model for the simple fact that each mile of stream in fact is adjoined by two riparian forests rather than one, because of the simple fact that the stream invariably has two shorelines. In another case, a bright young landscape architect working for the Forest Service addressed a crowd concerned about logging proposals on the Flathead Range near the popular Jewel Basin hiking area. He argued that the cuts would be invisible from Kalispell, because these cuts would subtend an arc of no more than a certain number of degrees. Again a clever and mathematically inclined participant in the meeting was quick to point out that the moon could be classed under the same mathematical criterion yet he could clearly see it from Kalispell, weather permitting. On another occasion it was the citizens of Wallace, Idaho, who took the lead in the commemoration of the hundredth anniversary of the 1910 fires that blazed through the Inland Northwest. This small group of dedicated individuals found the grant money to restore the trails to the Nickerson Adit where Ranger Edward Pulaski made his heroic stand against the fiery holocaust saving the lives of the bulk of his crew. The Nickerson Adit and the trail of Pulaski's retreat from the flames is most hallowed ground to anybody who has hefted the namesake tool invented by Ranger Pulaski and gone onto the line to fight fire. Yet these places remained largely unmarked and little noticed by the Forest Service until the populace of nearby Wallace made an issue of this fact and did the work that recognizes the historic importance of these places. The Forest Service's conduct prior to the issue being raised is nearly parallel to the unimaginable prospect of the military forgetting the location and meaning of the Arlington Cemetery.

Given the progression that continues today with less hands-on knowledge by the leadership and shrinking budgets, it is fair to ask where has the Forest Service gone and why? Where has the agency charged to manage arguably the greatest resource that one of this country's greatest presidents, Teddy Roosevelt, bequeathed in perpetuity to the American public gone? The agency charged to nurture these lands, to conserve these lands, and to protect these lands is too often missing in action as the herd of corporate and mechanized America chews these lands up. Why when you enter a remote ranger station in Eastern Oregon and ask about a trail in a wilderness prominent on the district does the staff give you a response of "Do I look like I hike?" Some of the answers are complex and tied to the changing tide of the country's pastimes and also to the general importance of these forest reserves to the corporate interests of the United States. This work attempts to find at least some answers by going back to the foundations of the Service and the flaws that a hundred years later create the instability that has resulted in the malaise the agency suffers today. Uncovering the flaws is an initial step in the recovery of an agency worthy of managing the stupendous resource our forebears bestowed on today's forest users. Public support for the correct and balanced management of these lands in which all Americans have an interest stake is the pathway to perpetuation of these forests as a national treasure.

Roosevelt's Legacy

On a recent ski trip into the mountains above Wallace, Idaho, a companion remarked on a treasure many westerners take for granted at least and recklessly abuse at worst. Where else, she remarked, could you ski up a mountain on the federal estate, through subalpine forest with the good possibility of encountering at least the tracks of the animals that represent all the natural native fauna of these mountains: deer, elk , moose, bobcat, lynx, pine marten, fisher, possibly a wolverine and wolves? Where else but in much of the western United States is this treasure looked upon nearly as a birth right? This is the treasure often taken for granted that a very few men exercising initiative and tools of their office bequeathed to our citizens. These national forest lands are a uniquely American idea emulated around the globe.

Typically, only historical scholars, biographers, a few conservationists, and a few interested others appreciate the confluence of personality, vision, and appropriate timely action at a key moment in our nation's history that bequeathed this legacy of national forests to the country. This author will not attempt the analysis and biography of this legacy's primary promoter, Theodore Roosevelt. Teddy Roosevelt's biography and contributions to our history are ably and comprehensively chronicled by historians and biographers exceedingly more capable than the author (1-4). Although central to the historical figure's conservation activity, the national forests and Forest Service are only a small piece of a much larger legacy left us by one of the four greatest men to occupy the presidency. This author's synthesis from those much more in depth treatments will have to suffice to understand the impetuous and forward inertia Roosevelt gave the national forests and the Forest Service.

A well understood fact of all mature persons is that no matter the station to which one is born, adversity will find its way into nearly everyone's life. Theodore Roosevelt was born into privilege as the first son of a successful New York merchant. His adversity was a frail and sickly constitution as a child. His weak physical being housed one of the exceptional scientific and political minds of American history. His was a mind influenced deeply by the work ethic and compassion for the less fortunate fostered by his father and the love of nature and the outdoors fostered at an early age by his uncle Rob Roosevelt. The luxury of travel as a youth to Europe and Egypt provided a world view at an early age. Travel in Europe provided the certain knowledge that large swaths of his country was still largely unaffected by man's activities. Yet it was the adversity of a frail constitution and his superior mind's ability to overcome that adversity that forged the exceptional personality of Teddy Roosevelt.

Teddy Roosevelt's father impressed upon his young mind the ability of a frail body to undermine a productive life. Without vigorous health to carry the mind forward, the soul is in many ways limited from full expression. The child born into relative luxury into America's commercial upper class made it his first mission in life to defy his bodily weakness and build himself up into a healthy vigor. He undertook the task with the vigorous enthusiasm that was a core and winning trait that served him through life. Not only did young Ted Roosevelt achieve his vision of robust health, but he surely learned the much greater truth that the mind is most often capable of achieving any end that it envisions. The lesson is learned and relearned by all high achievers. Teddy Roosevelt was one of our highest achievers in beneficial acts accomplished. At the core of his achievement lay the simple reverse of logic from why I cannot, the explanation, to why I cannot, the question, that leads invariably to the solutions that provide the means to nearly all reasonable ends. Through a number of adversities, some as great as the loss of his father and beloved spouse and mother on the same day and well before their natural time, Teddy found a productive and useful path forward driven by an exceptional intellect and an uncompromising will to achieve the ends he envisioned.

Roosevelt's other great influence was the American outdoors. The natural world as unspoiled as possible became the arena in which he pitted his growing physical strength against an implacable, unrelenting, and unforgiving force. Whether trips to the still wild lands of northern Maine as a student, or later in life as a cattle rancher in the demanding badlands of North Dakota, Teddy melded his desire for physical exertion with a deep interest in all manner of wild creatures. The fascination with nature was a passion from childhood encouraged and fostered by his Uncle Rob, himself an early conservationist. As a young man Roosevelt's initial desire was to be a naturalist, until civil service and politics demonstrated to him a possibility to achieve far more improvements in the society of which he was a part. Roosevelt, the observing naturalist, like other similar thinkers of his day, soon made the connection between viable wildlife populations and the habitat necessary to support them. In the same period of our history, the portion of North America governed by the United States was reaching the end of the settlement phase from coast to coast. The vision of unlimited land and resources was rapidly diminishing. Although the end was not at hand because broad expanses of the western lands remained open, the end could now be envisioned by forward thinking individuals.

The protection of the Adirondacks by New York, and Yellowstone by the Grant Administration were initial tentative political steps to meet the coming need to preserve at least some small part of the American landscape. The Forest Reserve withdrawals were endorsed by Congress in the Forest Reserve or Creative Act of 1891. Presidents Cleveland and McKinley created forest reservations addressing the growing realization that forest land required protection and some management to supply future timber to a fast growing nation. Yet all these early steps were tied to human needs for recreation and lumber. The primary motivation for the Adirondacks and Yellowstone reserves or the designation of Yosemite as a park by California, was as parks for human enjoyment of the scenery. This was a novel act worldwide in its time, to provide special places for the enjoyment of the entire populace, rather than for an aristocratic few, but the reasons behind the protections still centered on human needs. Likewise the Forest Reserves were primarily about providing a constant supply of lumber for construction, with little regard to the habitat protected within them. The later more massive withdrawals of lands into Forest Reserve protection by the Roosevelt Administration represented a philosophical shift to landscape and wildlife habitat protection.

Through service initially as a state legislator, civil servant, loyal servant to the Republican Party, Spanish-American War hero, and popular reformist Governor of New York state, Teddy Roosevelt rose to national prominence. During the same period, he developed a writing career with his emphasis on history, natural history, and the field sports-especially hunting. Politically Roosevelt was a progressive and reformist. He recognized the benefits of industrialization and business combinations in the creation of efficiencies, greater production, and rapid increase in the standard of living for all Americans. He as clearly recognized the corporate power created, the excesses of trade restraint and exploitation of workers. Through his political career he opposed these darker sides of industrial expansion. A political maneuver to rid New York of its populist reforming governor by installing Teddy as vice president resulted instead to his ascendency to the presidency when an assassin's bullet felled President McKinley. The reformist Roosevelt was now in the highest office in the land and was more than a political match for the reactionary forces in Congress and his own Republican Party that opposed him.

Teddy Roosevelt's initial departure from the conservation actions of his predecessors was the designation of wildlife refuges under the authority of the newly enacted Antiquities Act. Designation of the Pelican Island Reserve was distinctive in the fact that an area was set aside, not primarily for the use of man, but for the breeding of bird species. The maintenance of a wildlife population through protection of their breeding area was elevated above human use of this small plot of land. Roosevelt went on to designate fifty-one wildlife refuges during his tenure as president. Most often these protected wildlife breeding areas but at times these designations protected special ecosystems on which wildlife relied. In a similar manner, the national park system was expanded with the addition of five new parks and many monuments, not just for recreational opportunities for the American public, but to preserve special landscapes, wildlife habitat, or historical sites to inspire the public.

Unlike his predecessors, Teddy did not view the nation's natural resources from the comfort of the newly constructed oval office. Rather, as president he immersed himself in wild America often with its most ardent advocates. He traveled Yosemite and the Grand Canyon with John Muir, shedding the political entourage to hear around a campfire the first-hand accounts of the area from those who knew it best. He toured Yellowstone Park with a contingent of noted scientists and naturalists, men that were his peers in inquiry into nature. He famously hunted bear in Arkansas and did not allow his position to compromise his belief in the hunting ethic of the free chase. All his trips and tours were conducted in the public eye with full press coverage assured. Roosevelt was the first president to grasp not just the advocacy position vested in the presidency, the "bully pulpit," but the power of mass media as embodied in the press at that time to carry his message out to and to sell his ideas to the common citizen. In response to his energy, ideas, and his palpable concern for the common citizen, Theodore Roosevelt became one of the county's most popular presidents.

Although he was not the first president to add to the Forest Reserves, Roosevelt, with the heart of a field sportsman and the knowledge of a naturalist, was the first to recognize the value of the forest reserves in the conservation of broad sections of habitat that remained unspoiled. The other vehicles open to him, wildlife refuges and monuments, were too small to effectively protect habitat for the large land animals of the American continent. National parks required additional singular acts of congress which housed a business favoring plurality that opposed most set-asides of public lands. Western politicians whose districts contained the remaining broad areas of forest lands, in general vehemently opposed the protection of any additional federal land. Idaho's Senator Weldon Heyburn, whose political base was centered in the Coeur d'Alene Mining District, ranked in the forefront of congressmen opposing federal land reservations. Forest reserves could be designated by the president under the authority of the Forest Reserve Act. Withdrawal of forest reserves provided a direct means of protecting broad swaths of habitat from the highest mountain ridges to the valley bottoms and the frontage with the plains. From the perspective of the naturalist, which Roosevelt was, the forest reserve was not just a mechanism to save and manage forests, it was a mechanism to save the habitats on which the animals, and especially large land animals of North America relied. The elk could be accommodated from its summer haunts in the high mountain parks to its winter range on the south facing slopes of the sheltered valleys at low altitude. With the designation of national grasslands, the dream of re-establishing some buffalo herds could be envisioned and accomplished.

Many good arguments could be made for the conservation of forest lands. Rampant wildfires during the last decade of the nineteenth century and extending into the first two decades of the twentieth century highlighted to the public the need to designate and protect forests to assure wood production for the nation's future. Issues like fire protection, prevention of timber theft, and management superior to that of the timber industries' treatment of eastern forests developed the support to withdraw forest reserves. Roosevelt looked further into the future with at least some understanding of the fledgling and yet unnamed science of ecology. He understood the value of the national forests to the very integrity of the American environment.

Roosevelt used his presidential power to withdrawal hundreds of thousands and then millions of acres predominantly in the west where the federal estate remained extensive, into the Forest Reserves. The very scope of his forest reservation alarmed the business community and outraged western politicians. The business community expressed its concerns through its influence in Congress. Congress moved to remove the president's authority to withdrawal federal lands into forest reservations. Roosevelt had served a term as a state legislator and fully understood the deliberative pace of a legislative body compared to the speed at which an executive governmental branch could act. He understood as well that he must sign legislation for it to take effect. In a now celebrated last minute effort, Roosevelt and his chief forest aid Gifford Pinchot marked up maps on the White House floor and drew up descriptions of another and final round of forest reserve designations. The Forest Reserves were proclaimed just before Roosevelt bowed to the will of congress and signed the legislation removing his authority. By the end of his presidency 148 million acres well over 2.3 hundred thousand square miles were reserved within the national forests. His withdrawal of the vast expanse of land that became the national forest system is a model of visionary statesmanship. Roosevelt made the correct decision and took the appropriate actions to leave a legacy treasured by generations of his countrymen yet unborn. The expanded forest reserves were created despite a hostile majority in Congress representing the narrow business interests rather than the general public.

The national forests east of the Mississippi were almost an afterthought. By 1900 nearly all of the federal estate was west of the Rocky Mountain's Front Range. The forest reserves except for those in northern Minnesota, Wisconsin, Michigan, and New England were withdrawn in the west. Some national forest was created in the more boreal forest of the northern lake states and northern New England. There was a vision in the Forest Service for national forests in the largely privately owned eastern deciduous and Appalachian Mountain forests. As forest properties became commercially available, in large part during the depression years of the 1930s, the national forests of the east were purchased. Many of these forests reflect the patchwork nature of their repurchase origins. These lands were often in hilly country of the Appalachians where agriculture was marginal and the timber value had been cut out. Due to their already limited nature, cutover condition and proximity to large population centers, these eastern forests were managed with a different and somewhat more conservative strategy than their much more extensive counterparts in the west. These forests have been rebuilt in the intervening eighty years. Timber harvest had far less the emphasis while forest establishment, health, and recreation received more emphasis. The eastern forest covers a minor component of the landscape as compared to those of the west. These lands comprise no more than a small percentage of the land in states like Indiana or Kentucky, while in the west the federal estate can range to 70-80% of a state's landmass, with national forests being a significant percentage of the federal estate.

Roosevelt, always a man of action, took the appropriate actions that define our country's still deep seated will to preserve its natural heritage. Those immediately following him and certainly his distant cousin Franklin Roosevelt, followed his vision. The habitat necessary to perpetuate into the future the remarkable biota of the mid-latitudes of the continent was preserved intact primarily in the west, but with contributions across the country. The entire character of the west was preserved in large part by his actions. Field sportsmen and all forest users for generations and many yet to come can attribute their enjoyment of these lands to foresighted men and one man in the proper place and time with the will to buck the prevailing short sighted majority in congress that was influenced by a relatively minor but powerful group.

Managing the National Forest Legacy

Once created the greatly expanded forest reserves now required management and protection. These reserves existed in a region and at a time where resources were taken for personal use with little thought to legal procurement. The exploitation, waste, and misuse did not evaporate with the forest reservations designation. Western interests especially were accustomed to using the timber, minerals, water, and forage resources on the federal domain at either no or minimal costs. There was no authority on the ground to monitor or regulate such use. Forest fires seemed rampant during the summer months of the last decade of the nineteenth and first decade of the twentieth century, especially in cut-over lands.

An agency was necessary to manage the forest reserves and good knowledgeable men to staff that agency, especially on the ground. Prior to 1905 the Department of Interior was charged with this task of managing the forest reserves. Interior was woefully undermanned to accomplish the work. The Forest Reserve Transfer Act created the U. S. Forest Service in 1905 within the Department of Agriculture. The Forest Service assumed the Department of Interior's responsibilities for management of the forest reserves. Roosevelt placed his chief lieutenant and longtime conservation ally, Gifford Pinchot, at the head of the agency.

The rank and file to man the Forest Service was as odd a mix as the Rough Rider Regiment of the Spanish American War. Like the regiment, the Service started out as an exclusive and prestigious core, practically a club, at its inception. The early Forest Service personnel was a mix of college graduates and practical outdoorsmen schooled in the American west. Many of the college graduates were drawn from Yale's School of Forestry. Men like Fred Silcox, Elders Koch, and Joe Halm were forestry graduates schooled in the German or European model of forest management. Men like Fred Herrig, a former wrangler, Rough Rider and personal friend of Roosevelt, Edwin Pulaski, and Bill Rock were rough and tumble westerners schooled by the hard business of surviving in the now passing frontier west. These men had no concepts of forest management, but knew how to take and implement orders effectively and most importantly how to deal effectively with their fellow westerners accustomed to taking from the forest resources what they wanted. Emile Grandjean was an exception. Swiss and schooled in Europe as a forester, he came to the Idaho's rugged Sawtooth Mountains to mine, hunt and trap. After several years in the wilds, he joined the Forest Service and rose to the level of forest supervisor.

These men, whether college educated or practically educated, could develop a dedication to a cause and follow through on that dedication with results. The successes of the early Forest Service and its perseverance in the face of at times, monumental adversity was borne on the shoulders of these initial Forest Service employees. These early men created the tone that reached down to the Roan Anderson rangers of the fifties and sixties. The tone was palpably sensed by anyone who dealt with these men. The spirit of these men was most ably stated by brilliant Montana author, Norman Maclean. Maclean was a seasonal veteran of the Forest Service during the First World War years when "boys took the places of men in the woods." His character, the legendary Selway Ranger, Bill Bell, states the creed simply as "Men that love the woods without thinking they own them." Unfortunately a different tone of specialization, management to expediencies, career building, and aloofness from the resources on the ground has seriously eroded away the effective management of the nation's forests.

Those early rangers drawn from the remaining western pioneers possessed an intimate knowledge of the forests and a steadfast dedication to their duties. Ed Pulaski is a model example of both traits. On the day the great conflagration of the 1910 fire, the big blowup, Pulaski started in Wallace, which was a relatively safe location. By the afternoon he was astride the St. Joe Divide west of Moon Pass with two packers. With his experience he could clearly recognize that the fires fanned by a Palouse wind along the summit were merging into a massive fire front. When the packers turned back to run from the coming fire storm, Pulaski traveled on to the fire front to gather his crew. He successfully gathered the panicked men in the smoke and confusion. Many believed their salvation lay in the waters of nearby Elsie Lake. Pulaski knew the lake and its surroundings well. He had named the lake after his daughter. He was well aware of the cliff slope the refugees would be required to traverse down the alpine lake's cirque wall. He knew that in the darkness created by gathering dusk and the fire smoke, many of the crew, if not all, would fall to their deaths. Instead he quickly deduced that the fire would slow on the more barren east slopes of Striped Peak giving his crew possibly enough time to slip down the West Fork of Placer Creek to safety in Wallace. Should the fire front catch the crew as it did, be knew more immediate refuge could be obtained in the tunnel of the War Eagle Mine. When the fire moved too fast to allow even this refuge, Pulaski knew of and found in the darkness and flame the Nickerson Adit, which provided a safe refuge for most of his crew. Ed Pulaski's dedication to his crew and intimate knowledge of the landscape saved most of the men's lives. His dedication did not end when the danger was passed and his men were led back to Wallace. Through the rest of his Forest Service career and to the end of his life Pulaski lobbied an indifferent Forest Service bureaucracy to assist the crewmen whose health was damaged by the smoke and heat of the 1910 fire.

The early on-the-ground work of the Forest Service involved very little forest harvest. The priority then was forest protection, especially from fire. Establishing cabins and lookouts, building trail and the communication systems necessary to patrol the districts, and patrolling the forest to halt timber theft, illegal squatting and numerous other violations, was the initial work of the men in the field. The Timber and Stone Act permitted timber claims in the federal forest reserves up to 160 acres that, when "proved up" on in four years, could be purchased for $2.50 per acre. The law designed for woodlots on the Great Plains was heavily employed in prime forest land like that of Idaho's St. Joe Valley. The law reserved the timber for the personal use of the claimant and specially prohibited sale to lumber companies. However, many saw the advantage of proving up on a timber claim and then selling it to a timber concern. Early in its management of the forests, tremendous energy was expended governing timber claims. The great 1910 fire extinguished most St. Joe timber claims by leveling the forest, if not killing the claimant outright.

During the summer months detection and suppression of forest fires became the nearly all consuming activity of Forest Service personnel. Fire seasons such as that of 1910 consumed all the agency's attention and resources. As late as the 1930s Roosevelt's cousin, FDR, built up forest resources in the Civilian Conservation Core projects designed to give young Americans work. Trees were planted in burned areas, trails, cabins and lookouts were built or expanded and roads extended for forest access. Forest Service budgets were large, but mainly for the ultimate purpose of providing a work opportunity for young workers economically displaced by the depression. The net benefit was to the national forests. Franklin Roosevelt knew where and how to invest in the country.

On occasion, sales of timber were floated to the public in the early years, but federal forest land timber sales had a serious disadvantage as compared to logging on private lands. Most all of the forest reserve, the national forest land, was in mountainous terrain. By the time of the large lands withdrawals into the forest reserve system, most if not all of the flat bottom forested land in the valleys of the west had been homesteaded or purchased from the government in some manner. Timber claims were staked under the Homestead and Timber and Stone Acts, proved up on and although illegal, sold to large timber companies. Much of the Lazy Creek watershed north of Whitefish

Lake was transferred to private ownership in this manner. The Great Northern Railroad sent its agents west to buy homesteads in the forested land north of the lake. Once purchased the land was deeded over to the railroad. By this means the railroad secured the timber it would require for ties. Large sections of Idaho's St. Joe Valley, with its valuable stands of western white pine were claimed and later sold to Potlatch and a fewer lesser timber companies. Timber on this relatively flat bottomed or hill sloped land was far easier to harvest and transport to nearby mills with the equipment of those days than the harvest of the primarily mountainous national forests. Hence timber to supply the demand in the west and beyond flowed from the private domain, with modest interest expressed in federal timber.

There were exceptions. One exception was fire killed timber. A considerable volume of timber was harvested from the St. Joe Valley after the 1910 fire devastated many prized white pine stands. Such timber was sold at bargain prices because it was a perishable item which would decay beyond use ("check out") in most cases within 2 to 5 years. Another exception was the Coeur d'Alene River's Little North Fork. Untouched by the 1910 fires, it contained stands of nearly 90% white pine. Beginning shortly after the 1910 salvage logging, Diamond Match Company began logging in the Little North

Fork. The logging was supported by a railroad system to remove logs over Burnt Cabin Summit and down a grade to the Rathdrum Prairie. The logging proceeded under the Forest Service's watchful eye into the 1950's. The result of the removal of white pine without its regeneration due to blister rust infection, is the widespread "high graded" stands now dominated by the white fir and hemlock left behind with the addition of Douglas fir that grew from seed in the more open areas.

Generally however, relatively low volumes were harvested from the forest lands well into the 1920s and by the time some demand for federal timber was developing, the bottom fell out of the national economy in the 1930s erasing much of the demand for raw timber. During this period many timber companies went bankrupt. During and increasingly so after the Second World War federal timber became a mainstay in the timber supply picture.

Even at its inception a management flaw was planted in the Forest Service and another was seeded by the traumatic 1910 fire season. The flaw was adherence to European forest management model, which Gifford Pinchot studied abroad and was taught universally in the Yale Forestry School and the many university programs that modeled Yale's forestry program across the country. This flaw would take over 35 years, along with the demand for federal timber to increase dramatically before it surfaced to join forces with another management demand--timber harvest maximization. The flaw of near absolute or at least the attempt at absolute fire suppression would lie unrecognized even longer until plant community structures shifted and the long known value of fire in plant ecosystems was at last again recognized by agency management.

The European system of Forestry treated trees as a crop much like wheat or corn, but in this case for saw timber production. The crop took a much longer time span to mature, no doubt, but the central tenant is that a forest can be harvested by any number of harvest methods, trees can be planted back and these trees will grow to harvestable maturity. The growth cycle of trees in a managed forest stand is much shorter than that in an unmanaged wild stand. The trees retained for growth, not thinned out, are those with superior characteristics. The trees of the managed stand are grown through their most productive years of wood accumulation, but once wood accumulation begins to stabilize at a lower rate (harvestable maturity) the trees are cut and new seedlings planted.

Silvicultural management is a great alteration from the natural growth of and development of a forest stand. In nature, typically some stand replacing event like fire

33

removes all or most of the living trees. Yet the larger woody debris of the dead trees remains. The remaining boles either stand or lie on the forest floor creating habitats for many species of plants and animals including seedling trees. Root sprouting shrubs and forbs occupy the site while trees' seedlings establish over a short or longer period. The trees grow to overtop the shrubs and forbs and prosper through a period of rapid wood accumulation. Eventually minor fires, wind, and disease thin the stand while dominant individuals capture a greater part of the stand's light and nutrient resources. The stand differentiates with older individuals interspersed with younger trees growing in the openings created by the demise of the earlier trees of the stand. The natural stand reaches a diverse and dynamic equilibrium with heterogeneity of tree of species and age. Trees are living and dead, erect or fallen and damaged. Diverse habitats are created by the diversity of trees in a diversity of life stages. The many habitats create living space for the multitude of organisms that inhabit the forest. Banked in these old growth stands is a great deal of wood biomass (timber) that can be harvested, but once, until the long cycle necessary to create old growth is again repeated.

Managed timber stands are typically nurtured, the undesirable trees removed, and space provided so that an even larger timber crop might be harvested than would have been under natural conditions.

Fertilization and spraying of herbicides and pesticides might be practiced to guard the health of the desired wood producing trees. The goal is timber production, while any additional resource values are held as secondary benefits to this primary purpose. The difference is as stark between a forest community full of different life forms and a rather monotonous tree farm's low diversity. Plant ecologists would classify a forest as the diverse community, while the tree farm more ecologically resembles the early seral stage of a developing forest.

Silviculture through this timber production approach, like any simplified management scheme with prescriptive methods, may work on some species in some locations for some time. However, when its extremities or even its subtle tenets are applied over the breadth and scope of environments that the national forest system encompasses, failures can be expected. One example is its application to high altitude subalpine spruce forests of the intermountain west. Bark beetle epidemics occurred primarily in Colorado's White River Plateau during and after the Second World War. At the time the government's attention was focused on the war and no resources were available to combat the outbreaks. After the war the spruce bark beetle epidemics in a geographically small area were used as an excuse to clear cut high altitude spruce forests throughout the intermountain west. The fact soon was established that the spruce could not be planted back as seedlings. Any spruce left to bear seed did not produce sufficient seedlings for regeneration of the species. In locations where trees occupy a site prior to the dominant spruce, seral species, like lodgepole pine and aspen colonized the environments the spruce seedlings, once re-established, could again survive. The time frame, however, from seedling to harvestable spruce was greatly lengthened by the inability of spruce seedlings to prosper and grow in high light intensity environment created by clear cutting. Additional problems like the dominance of shrub species for extended periods after cutting that slows a return to the trees' growth and production, removal of forest canopy from habitats where the canopy itself made possible the forest reproduction and the threat of insect and other disease infestation in tree monocultures, are but a few problems with the idealized model of fiber production under the European inspired methodology. Broadcast use of pesticides, herbicides, and even rodenticides were made to correct these problems, but seldom was the core belief in this system of silviculture questioned in the decades from the 1950s into the 1970s.

When the model failed to produce the expected outputs, the difference was made up with another theoretical sleight of hand: deflation of the rotation period to allow inflation of the harvest. The rotation period is the time required for seedlings to mature into harvestable trees. If it is shortened it is logical the cut can be increased. A forester trained in a well-respected west coast forestry school would tell you the rotation period for Douglas fir on the coast is eighty years, while the forest ecologist who was housed elsewhere on the university campus and spent his career studying these forests, would place the number closer to 125 years. Accounting measures as rotation deflation can mislead investors and congressmen, but natural systems remain unimpressed and largely on their own time tables. Hence many areas of the Pacific Coast and elsewhere, later and more generally were cut out of their supply of old growth and the new harvestable trees were not there to maintain the industry. Mills closed.

Research work beginning in the 1970s on the H.J. Andrews Experimental Forest sponsored, in large part by the Forest Service, came to fruition in the next two decades. These studies compared the old growth Douglas fir forest to the tree farms created over much of the west coast. The research findings are summarized in Luoma's work; "The Hidden Forest" (5). The work demonstrated that trees play a role through the entire cycle of the forest well after they die and fall to the forest floor. The cycling of nutrients, the building of soil, and the creation of the diverse habitats that foster the web of life on which the large land mammals of mid-latitude North America are suspended, are all fostered in the old growth forest and spectrum of forests developing towards old growth. These same conditions are diminished in the monoculture tree farms.

The H.J. Andrews and other research demonstrated yet another more important clear fact. A forest is more than a collection of trees growing on a site conducive to their culture. A forest is a far more complex interdependent ecosystem nurturing a large host of life forms plant, animal, and microbial. The linkages between these species interdependency are built up over long periods as a site moves through the succession cycle gradually progressing from one phase to the next. A tree farm is just that a plot of land dedicated to tree growth. Harvestable trees might be attainable in the rotational periods silviculturalists profess, but a forest takes much longer to grow and become mature. When radio spots speak of "working forest", the reference is to tree farms not true forest. Tree farms are an appropriate land use on private and possibly state lands so designated constitutionally, but the nation was promised forest for national forest land and that promise must be honored.

Often the historical conclusion is made that Theodore Roosevelt favored wise use of the forests but with use, as opposed to protection, as interpreted by Muir and other preservationists of the time. Certainly, based on the knowledge of his time, he was a believer in the theory of forest management brought over from Europe by Pinchot and others. Yet at his core, Theodore Roosevelt was a naturalist and a scientific inquirer into nature. Certainly one of his primary goals for the vast forest reserves was to maintain populations of the large fauna of North America. If the naturalist and hunter, Theodore Roosevelt, had the opportunity to review the current body of science indicating that tree farms will not sustain a diverse environment, a very different basic approach and instructions may have been issued to the fledgling Forest Service in terms of timber harvest. As the history unfolded it was an aware American public that demanded change in management of the nation's forests.

The second flaw lingering in the U. S. Forest Service's management direction was its approach to fire. The forest reserves were authorized through the Forest Reserve Act. A good deal of the stimulus for the legislation was the rampant wild fires throughout the country especially in the south, northeast, and upper Midwest. The intensity of many of these fires was attributable to poor management of the slash created by timber harvest. Fire in the west was a minor issue in the last decade of the nineteenth century simply due to the small population affected. In the northeast, upper Midwest and southeast, forest fires were a large issue, because it was in these locations where timber was harvested and a substantial population lived in the countryside burned.

The Forest Service took over fire control responsibilities for the forest reserves from the Department of Interior after its 1905 inception. The poor timber harvest slash practices that intensified forest fires in the northeast, upper Midwest and southeast were not changed and large wildfires persisted in these regions until better practices were implemented. The 1910 fire season was the formative event for the Forest Service's subsequent fire policy for the next ninety years. Fires burned in 1910 all around the West as well as in the upper Midwest. The great burn of North Idaho and Northwest Montana eclipsed all the others in size and impact on the Forest Service. A line can be drawn down the Bitterroot Divide from Clark Fork Idaho to Moose Creek in the Selway Wilderness, a distance of 160 miles. On either side of that line for an average of twenty-five miles fire damaged the Coeur d'Alene, St Joe, Kaniksu, Kootenai, Lolo, Clearwater and Bitterroot Forests. As much as 70% of the area had suffered stand replacement fire, blackening the earth for thousands of square miles. Loss of life among firefighters pressed into service by the Forest Service, prospectors, hunters and trappers, timber claimants, and homesteaders scattered over the landscape was great. The actual loss of lives can only be estimated. The mining boomtown of Wallace that had hosted Teddy Roosevelt just a few years earlier was a third consumed, while whole towns like Taft and Grand Forks were erased from the map. Much of the fire burned sparsely populated wilderness. In its initial full-fledged attack on wild fire, the Forest Service was routed. The trails and communications systems necessary to attack small fires early did not exist.

The strong Palouse wind that caused the blow up could not have been countered even by today's technology. The Sundance fire of 1967 in Idaho's Selkirk Range clearly demonstrated that even with advanced firefighting technology, a fire driven by a Palouse wind across the forests of North Idaho is unstoppable. What is only understood more recently from the fire histories that science has developed for most of the western forest, is that the great 1910 fire was not an unusual stand replacing fire event. Similar fires of similar size raged in the Coeur d'Alene and adjacent mountains periodically long before the influence of European man. A great fire of similar scope struck the western areas of the Coeur d'Alene Mountains in the mid-seventeenth century. Subsequent great fires as the Half Moon fire of 1929, Sleeping Child of 1961, the Sundance fire of 1967, Yellowstone of 1988, Biscuit Fire of 2002 and most recently the Bitterroot Valley fires of 2004 demonstrate that the potential for great conflagrations is always present in the mature forests of the Northwest awaiting only the proper weather conditions and an ignition. Anyone who has ever hefted a Pulaski and went out to fight these fires can tell you that the Forest Service with its bulldozers, tankers, airdrops, and manpower does not extinguish a great fire—only the onset of winter does.

Lacking the wisdom that the 1910 fire was an unstoppable force of the natural order of life, the Forest Service went to work to limit if not eradicate fire from the national forests. A trail system, fire chasers to follow those trails seeking out fires, lookouts manned by brave souls spending a summer isolated, and a telephone communication system were installed in the years after the 1910 burn. Wild firefighting equipment improved with the Pulaski, water packs, tankers and areal slurry planes. Specialized, firefighting teams as Hotshots and Smokejumpers were organized, trained, and deployed. An entire incident command system adopted today for most emergency events was developed. The Forest Service was successful in suppressing fires before these could mushroom into unmanageable conflagrations. Although the great fires listed above and others slipped through the net, the Forest Service and sister agencies were so successful in fire suppression that the role of fire, and especially the small fire, in shaping the flora and therefore the fauna of the west and elsewhere was greatly negated.

Worse, more recent ecological science pointed to the fact that suppression of the small fire only fed the eventual size and intensity of the inevitable next great fire.

The role of fire in the western environment was recognized by Muir and others before the science of ecology had a name. Periodic fire was known to maintain certain forest stands. Trees like the long leaf, lodgepole, and jack pines were known to have adapted their reproductive strategies to fire, while long-lived seral species as the tamarack, ponderosa pine, and Douglas fir were known to develop thick bark to retard the impacts of fire. Most forest undergrowth shrubs had developed root crown from which they could sprout after fire damage. Natural science and ecology were speaking for a century of the important role of fire in the forest ecosystem as the Forest Service and timber industry ignored the message for nearly eighty years and sought to fully suppress fire. Only when the science pointed to the fuel loading aspects of total fire suppression and the Forest Service had many years of experience control burning its timber harvest units, did the policy change away from full fire suppression.

Although the Forest Service now recognizes the place of fire in the forest ecosystem and uses it as a management tool, the specter of fire still haunts the agency. The Forest Service and a large number of its employees remain addicted to the thrill of the fire fight. Employees that have retired are drawn back each summer to man forest fire overhead teams. The money is good, but the addiction robs them of other joys of a short summer. A whole infrastructure of the Forest Service remains dedicated to fire suppression and is employed as quickly as possible when the occasion arises. Certainly, there is a need to protect life and property against the force of wild fire in the forests and grasslands. However, many believe the Forest Service is too quick to spend its time and treasure on this new priority again over all others including proper management of the forests. The agency uses wild fire suppression as a key argument for its value to the citizen, while the employees are drawn to the long hours of overtime pay. The agency will not spend federal funds entrusted to it on any project other than fire suppression off of the lands it manages. As an example, numerous mine and mill sites located in the Prichard Creek drainage of North Idaho eroded mine wastes from national forest land onto private property further downstream. The agency would address the wastes on the lands it managed, but steadfastly refused to address the wastes on the private land that had their origins on the federally managed lands. Idaho was asked to find the funding to address these wastes. However, a wild fire threatening residential property or recreational cabins is fought without regard to property boundaries and that residential or recreational property is given top priority for protection from the fire.

It is not argued here that the Forest Service should not respond to and assist the combat wild fire with the potential to injure the public or private property. It should, but with more restraint than is currently applied. Too often the urban interface is so liberally interpreted that cabins or homes far distant from any other structures or towns are pointed to as the reason for suppression. Far too often a significant portion of the agency's budget is consumed fighting fire to protect recreational homes of the nation's most wealthy citizens rather than expending those funds on the forest for all the citizens. The Beaver Creek Complex fire fight of the summer of 2013 is but one example. The fire was given the highest priority in Idaho and received the most resources during July and August of the year because it burned close to Ketchum, Idaho a playground of the most fortunate of the country. Owners of homes built in forested areas and those adjacent or in close proximity to the national forests take the risk of wildfire. In many, but not all cases, these are second or recreational homes of the more wealthy. If the private property owner of any means wants to improve that property near forests prone to fire, that individual should be responsible for their actions, not the federal taxpayer. There are other options ranging from insurance and mobile living quarters to private fire protection dependent on their means. The Forest Service and other agencies, federal and state should not subsidize their choices. A greater portion of the Forest Service budget should be channeled to protection and enhancement management of the national forests, exclusive of fire.

The Forest Service created by Roosevelt to steward the national forest system created by his forest reservations and entrusted to Pinchot as it first chief had in its inception a deep seated management prejudice that was eventually rebelled against by a large segment of the American public. It was an infant agency when the Great Fire of 1910 etched a prejudice against any fire in the forest into its management fabric. Both of these problems rose to the surface in the late 1970s through the 1990s fostering tremendous change in the agency and the forest it manages.

Forest Service Subverted

An axiom of government is that the regulated entities eventually befriend and beguile the regulator. Both regulated and regulators are human. These individuals are thrown together by mutual if not confluent interest on a regular basis. Humanity, itself, is in part based on the development of empathy for the wishes and needs of others. Therefore it is not surprising that some commonality of vision should develop under these conditions. Once, this author was on business inspecting the water quality standards compliance of an eastern Idaho federal timber sale of some fairly dismal logs from a North Idaho perspective. The harvest was implemented by a low budget "gypo" logger whose family camped alongside his workplace. The Forest Service project manager remarked how happy she was to see the logger get the current load of logs out so he could provide food for his family. The humanity and sincerity of the manager is unquestionable. Her empathy for the family was understandable to anybody with a heart. Yet a similar confluence of sentiment and goals developed between logging companies and the Forest Service's planners and harvest regulators during the fifties to the detriment of the national forests.

As timber production from the national forests became an important part of the national timber supply after the Second World War, the relationship between the timber industry and Forest Service especially at the upper supervisory levels and in Congress became closer. Timber production and regeneration of harvestable and desirable timber became the most important goal of the agency's mission. Even the firefighting imperative was recast in terms of protection of the managed forest and timber production, rather than protection of the forests. The legacy of that recast message is the all too often refrain of the timber industry and its political allies today. These groups argue the national forest are unhealthy and fire prone, presumably because timber is not being harvested.

The timber cut from the forties to date was primarily all first cut forest. The promise of regeneration and forests to cut in the second and succeeding rotations was part of the rationale. However, the timber on the national forests should be viewed as the reserve banked for national timber production at a sustained yield. During these decades the national timber account was being withdrawn from the public's forest with the promise that it would be restored by new growth in a reasonable time frame, equaling a sustained yield. Sustained yield was an article of faith and forest management logic that promised that the new forest would be there to cut when the original growth forest was consumed. All the other resources were accounted for by the size and abundance of the forest. Watershed was protected in the managed forest. There were plenty of streams to fish, game to hunt, and undisturbed places to visit in the vast area of the national forests. Given the abundance of timber, water and recreational opportunities, the priority of the Forest Service during the mid-decades of the twentieth century was summoned up in the ranger's management direction of "get the cut out."

Even if a ranger sensed the cut was excessive and should be curtailed, there were officials further up in the forest supervisor's office to counter such sentiments. More often the supervisor's office now planned and put up the timber sales with input by the ranger district but, the final decision was not made at the forest ranger's level. If a ranger could prevail, concerning a cut, even higher political pressure was applied.

During the 1960s a blow down event in the lodgepole pine forest on the Redfeather District's Baldy Mountain's east face was transformed into a large timber cut. Trees that owed their genesis to a stand replacement fire likely set by the retreating Ute Tribe in the 1860s, had reached maturity, and natural events were beginning to transform the stand from a near monoculture of pine into a more diverse forest stand. The timber harvest that started as the salvage of blow down timber grew into an increasingly massive clear-cut into the mid-1960s. The timber stand improvement practice of cutting down any residual trees to retard the spread of dwarf mistletoe only added to the open vistas. After a series of additional blow downs at the cut's edge created by the stand's loss of resistance to the wind, Roan Anderson and his assistant district forester believed it was time to curtail the cut. Unfortunately, the two log mills down in Fort Collins had grown dependent on this source of timber. The mill managers complained to the local congressional representative who in turn lodged the complaint with the upper management of the Forest Service. From that level the command to get out more cut from the area came down to the forest and district staff. The cutting went on. Forest management was practiced by political fiat rather than by methods of sustained yield as envisioned by the forest management model espoused by most foresters and the Forest Service.

Such management by demands of the mills was not uncommon throughout the national forests. Spruce beetle epidemics during the war years were used as the motivation to cut healthy subalpine spruce stands throughout the Rocky Mountain West. The cuts were pursued into the highest subalpine basins in the then most remote ranges of the Intermountain West.

Remote valleys and basins, even today in Montana's Whitefish Range, were cut right up to the cirque lakes at the very highest elevations. The backdrop for Ernest Thompson Seton's "Krag the Kootenai Ram" was cut nearly to the cliff's the bighorn sheep herd roamed. High elevation areas cut in the 1950s have failed to regenerate properly after sixty years. The western pine beetle that kills many of the individuals in lodgepole pine stands was the motivation for massive clear cuts throughout the West in the seventies and early eighties and in Western Canada today. Where such infestations to run their course without intervention, two of every three trees are killed opening the forest to other species as larch and spruce that take over stand dominance. An expanse of the Bitterroot Divide near Lookout Pass experienced pine beetle outbreaks in the first decade of the twenty-first century. The forest was not cut because it flanks Interstate 90 raising view issues. Dominance in the forest shifted to larch and spruce. The forest evolves and the timber resource lost was not huge. Even after legislation requiring much greater scrutiny of projects to salvage or harvest timber before some natural event, the motivation to cut timber based on a perceived threat remains a mainstay of national forest management. The most recent case is the "Fire Smart" Program where trees are cut in the name of fire prevention several miles from the nearest home requiring protection. A recent proposal to cut timber in the Coeur d'Alene Forest's upper Beaver Creek watershed invoked protection of the "urban interface" when the closest "urban interface" is six miles distant to the south over the ridge at Wallace. The programs of the 1950s and 1960s down to Fire Smart program of today demonstrate a strong prejudice in sectors of the Forest Service to cut trees and harvest timber. The prejudice is often times wrapped in the cloak of maintaining western community economic stability, but whatever guise it assumes, it goes back to the built-in flaw and strongly held belief by many foresters to this day that the forest can be managed as a crop like any other in man's agronomic fields without fundamentally altering the quality of the forest or its other resources. The history of massive cuts clearly demonstrated that cadres of foresters have been the strong proponents of timber harvest even to the detriment of other forest resources.

The cadre supportive of timber harvest maximization has a label in the Forest Service, natural resource management, and environmental management communities: timber beasts. The Forest Service was infiltrated by foresters with these motivations just as soon as timber on the public domain became an important part of the timber supply. From the 1950s well into the 1970s timber harvest was the primary purpose of the Forest Service. By whatever means and with the strong backing of the federal government the cut was maintained and the national forests were transformed from a balance of old growth timber into a balance of second growth timber. Even worse is the inventory of forest lands high-graded for the desirable timber species, while the less desirable species were left behind to dominate the stands. Stands of the Coeur d'Alene's Little North Fork are text book cases. Coupled with fire prevention efforts over an eighty year period, the result is generation of large expanses of forest of the shade tolerant less vigorous mature trees. Idaho's Coeur d'Alene Forest is a case study in management that led to this result and the resulting large acreages of stands of marginal productivity. Such stands have little wildlife value or diversity. Forest Service budgets were kept robust through much of this period but not to complete improvements as in the early years or in the dark days of the depression. Budgets were ample to maintain the timber cut.

By the late 1950s the Forest Service charged with protecting the forest was sufficiently infiltrated and controlled by foresters whose primary goal was getting the cut out that this became the primary goal of the agency. Congress shared in the goal wholeheartedly often basing the budget of the agency on the cut produced. Budget within the agency was allocated to those districts producing timber harvest. The rank and file professional employees fully understood that advancement depended on their ability to sustain the harvest. Methods were soon adapted to achieve the goals. Deals were provided to logging contractors to build the roads required and often timber was sold at bargain stumpage rates. Extreme cases involved subsidized timber sales, where the roads necessary to harvest the timber cost more than the timber harvested. In these cases, the timber is cut and essentially given away to build the roads that allowed access to the timber. Convincing arguments were made that the planted second growth, protected from insects and disease, thinned and even in cases fertilized, would mature faster into saw timber. This shorter time to harvest, although assumed rather than proven, provided the excuse to shift the yield (timber cut) upward. The cut was not of second growth but was additional initial cut forest. The capital was withdrawn from our forests over this period on the promise of higher interest rates which were never proven and did not accrue.

While Lassie and Smokey the Bear fronted for the Forest Service in advertisements we all viewed, and mostly believed, the forests seemed under good management, and the timber cut had its heyday. Annual cuts of hundreds of millions of board feet from the most productive Northwest Forests were common. Export of whole logs to Japan from Alaska's Tongass Forest created barren hillsides open to accelerated erosion. Many forests became so heavily covered by roads that tens of miles of roadway were common in a single square mile section of national forest. Free use of log collection systems like the Idaho jammer created parallel roads every 200 feet up mountain slopes. The Coeur d'Alene Forest gained the dubious distinction of being the most road heavy forest in the National Forest System from a rapacious thirst for timber to feed the mills in Coeur d'Alene and Post Falls. A cadre of Forest Service employees was more than willing to put up the timber sales to support the harvest.

To be fair, there were voices within the Forest Service opposed to prevailing timber harvest current. Gerry House was born in a log cabin near and grew up on the shores of Hayden Lake with a deep regard for the lake and its forested watershed largely managed by the Forest Service. Gerry's father scaled logs for the Forest Service at the Valley View station on the Ohio Match railroad grade. The railroad was a main transit route for logs harvested in the Little North Fork Coeur d'Alene River. As a young man Gerry trained as a forester, joined the Forest Service and rose through it ranks. He eventually became the forest planner for the Idaho Panhandle National Forests, which borders Hayden Lake. Gerry was well aware that harvest activities and the systems used were damaging the water resources. Hydrology and fisheries specialist reported their opinions and results to the planning chief. Always remaining within the confines of the agency, he took the case to the forest supervisor. After retirement the supervisor during Gerry's tenure publically stated that hardly a work morning would pass without Gerry in his office lobbying for resource protection. Working within the system, Gerry caused the agency no embarrassment and encouraged a shift in emphasis. The remedial steps required were developed by watershed specialists. Funds were found for the remedial work on damaged watersheds. Work began initially on a modest scale to remove forest haul roads that negatively affected the streams of the forest. Eventually, after his retirement, the work was completed on the Hayden and Yellowbanks Creeks Roads in the Hayden Lake watershed that Gerry cherished most. The removal of unnecessary and damaging forest roads took nearly fifteen years to accomplish, but the result was fast recovering watersheds and streams. The change began and grew because Gerry treasured the forests of his youth and changed mindsets at the upper management levels

Gerry House was not a totally rare exception. There were professional scientists, hydrologists, wildlife, and fisheries specialists, whose science demonstrated that the management for a single resource degrading another resource was in direct contradiction to the multiple use model the agency presented to the public. When their science and arguments began to develop traction, especially with the public exterior to the agency, such specialists found themselves reassigned to another forest, typically far away from their current assignment. If the post was not accepted, the individual had to seek employment elsewhere. A few of these protestors found those other means and remained local to voice their criticisms. There was little room for team members who bucked the prevailing direction of the Forest Service.

Management with a disproportionate emphasis on timber harvest is not an issue on the large forest land holdings of private timber companies as Potlatch, Boise Cascade, and Weyerhaeuser. Nor is it an issue on smaller holdings such as Pack River, Inland Empire Paper Company or the neighbor down the road with a tree farm. The national forests are the exception. These lands were stored for posterity to be managed for sustained forest values. All forest values, not just timber. The infiltration of the Forest Service with personnel whose primary motive was to harvest trees betrayed the promise. Forest condition reached such a point on forests like Oregon's Siuslaw, that one could discern the crossing from National Forest onto private land owned by Boise Cascade without the assistance of a map or sign. The condition of the forest was notably improved on the private industrial land. The National Forest in the mind of the industry leadership and evidently the Forest Service leadership was more expendable than the land in private ownership. The record immutably written on the lands the Forest

Service has managed supports the only conclusion possible: the Forest Service leadership betrayed the legacy of its founder, Theodore Roosevelt.

As long as the reserve of uncut and wild places remained abundant, the public could be beguiled by Lassie and Smoky the Bear public service ads. Near the end, even the venerable Raymond Burr was brought in to bolster the image. An unchanging dynamic however was creeping up on the status quo. The regeneration was not replacing the initial cuts as promised. More and more forest was transformed into cut-over lands, with less and less untouched forest for the other forest users. Other resources such as fish and wildlife habitat, water quality, and aesthetics were beginning to show the impacts of the one-dimensional management. River systems like the North Fork Coeur d'Alene River lost vast amounts of their fish habitat and the productivity of the fishery soon made this clear. Where fisherman once caught limits of cutthroat trout for many years, there were few trout remaining. Granted other factors exacerbated the problems, but the core issue of all resources diminished after timber cuts became more and more difficult to conceal from the public. A tour across most of the forest revealed a large expanses of clear cuts in various state of regeneration, but much of the land was clearly recognizable as cut over.

Forests of the west that like those of the east which once seemed a boundless resource, especially if scientific forestry was applied, had begun to appear ever increasingly less boundless. By the mid-1960s it was clear to many forest users that the storehouse of wild places was rapidly being cut up by roads and harvested in vast clear cut harvests. The realization of this loss predicted much earlier by John Muir and Bob Marshall was becoming more common.

Public Revolt

A vast number of ordinary middle class citizens enjoy an array of recreational pleasures in the national forests. A quick but chilly mountain stream crossing at the trailhead and a brisk twenty minute hike can transport one from the mechanized world of man's construction into the realm of an old growth forest. Tall cedars some five or six feet in diameter grow in a cove situated where the rushing stream brakes for a hundred yards into a gentler gradient and the narrow valley is wider for a short distance. On the hottest days the air is cooled and humidified by the mountain stream. Large Douglas fir, white pine and white fir intermix with the cedars. The stand is open with shafts of sunlight reaching onto the forest floor. The litter of fallen trees and tree parts cover its floor. The boles of fallen giants dam and redirect the stream flow. The tracks of elk, moose and deer attest to its use by large animals, while the songs of birds and chirp squirrels attest to smaller wildlife present. The old growth community only hints at its diversity while its ancient character is indisputable.

This place is one of a million special places protected in our national forests. It is one of many special to this writer. Others treasure the hillsides of wildflowers fresh on a spring morning. Others, a near ridge top glen of oaks at sunrise with a flock of wild turkeys set to fly down from their nightly perch to begin the delicate dance of the spring turkey hunt. The fisherman casting across the trout stream flowing through national forest treasures the setting of his sport as important as the ever present chance a fish may rise to his fly. The clear cool waters fostered by the national forests are essential to the sport. Others treasure the trails leading up to the high peaks ascended with considerable effort to survey the country all about from the high perch. Many seek the huckleberry, morels, fall mushrooms and other wild foods in the forests. Some treasure and maintain the old fire lookouts replaced by modern technology but not in the hearts of those who revere the simpler old ways. The fall deer, elk and moose hunts are played out in innumerable hunting camps distributed across the national forests. For a large number these hunts highlight their year and mark a family or social tradition through time. The participants are transported to an earlier more elemental existence masked by modern living. The national forests in winter host numerous downhill skiers enjoying the scenery, the hiss of ski or board cutting through snow, and the thrill of the rapid run down. Many more skiers seek the more sedate setting of cross-country skiing on the forests while backcountry skiers venture far afield to ski mountainside slopes untrammeled by other skiers. Snow machine enthusiasts cruise large networks of groomed trails along the road systems in the national forests, while the more adventurous pit their skill and machines against steep mountain slopes. These and many more pursuits as varied as a simple stroll along a paved interpretive nature trail to a guided weeks long horseback trip into one of the great wilderness areas constitute the recreational use of the nation's forests.

All these experiences support the vary soul of the American people and the very quality of their lives. Some generate recreational economy for the businesses nearby, but their real value is not economic. The real value is in the mental and spiritual health of the people. These are resources made available to all with the means to reach these storehouses of simple pleasures. This value of the forests to the wellbeing of the whole of the public is of far greater value than timber, grazing or hydropower revenues that might be obtained. This recreational and spiritual resource should always be foremost in the minds of managers as the extractive resource management are considered. These irreplaceable storehouses of simple pleasures of life are and should remain the property of all the country's people held and managed in trust by the federal government through its Forest Service.

An educated public passionate about its forest experiences can be misled only for so long. Eventually it will recognize the truths bore out on the ground. The American public recognized the environmental problems affecting its quality of life in the late 1960s. Part of the change coming would fundamentally affect the Forest Service. By the 1960s the "get the cut out" policy was so engrained in the Forest Service hierarchy and Congress that many of the ranks of both could not see the storm coming. When the storm broke, Congress responsible to the public every two to six year received the message. The entrenched Forest Service hierarchy was another ten to fifteen years recognizing times had changed. Only the retirement of the old managers and a new crop of managers triggered the transition.

The public revolt concerning the environment in the late 1960s and early 1970s was hardly confined to the forest environment. A general recognition occurred that the environment of the country was rapidly degrading arose in the late 1950s and early 1960s, but took the required decade for public support to build for Congress to act. Kalispell smokejumper turned new frontiersman in the Kennedy administration, George Ostrom recognized the single resource management of the Forest Service in the late 1950s. At a late 1950s luncheon event given for the smokejumper core in Missoula, he was seated across from then Representative Mike Mansfield. The brash young man filled the representative's ears with his complaints about the Forest Service's one dimensional management. A few years later as President Kennedy took office and Mansfield rose to the Senate, George found himself tapped to go to Washington to help make changes. On a broader scale, Kennedy's Secretary of the Interior Stewart Udall was early to recognize and publish his views along with others on the damage to the environment. Yet these were the visionaries and not the general public. Another half decade or more was necessary for the public to catch up. Polluted streams, poor air quality, pesticide contaminated food, the recognition of species decline to agricultural practices and habitat loss all convinced the general public. Many westerners felt the loss of favored trails and campsites as these were logged over. Fishing streams once productive lost productivity as logging and road sediment impacts mounted.

By 1969 a sufficient part of the public was aroused and informed their congressional representatives that new management was necessary. The public told congress it wanted change and regulation. The governmental experts and interest groups who studied and understood the problems created the legislative solutions. Initially these changes were made with the Wilderness, Clean Water, and Clean Air Acts. Later the Resource Conservation and Recovery and Comprehensive Environmental Response, Compensation and Liability Acts would address solid and hazardous waste problems, while the Endangered Species Act would address species extinction.

The Forest Service's new direction from Congress came in the National Forest Management Act of 1976. The old approach of multiple use created as agency policy and most often interpreted in favor of timber harvest, was swept aside in favor of a forest planning process in which the interest groups and general public was given a strong voice. The management direction that the individual forests would follow for the lands these contained would be decided in a public process with the public and the various interest groups involved. Prudent forest management practices, public input, and the environmental laws prescribed by Congress would determine the general management plan. The plan would be the blue print for individual management decisions until the plan was routinely revised on a set schedule. Some practices such as clear cutting forest was expressly discouraged by limitation to opening of less than forty acres unless compelling justification could be made for larger forest openings. The Coeur d'Alene Forest's North Fork watershed was heavily clear cut from the 1950s through 1970s, but owing to the new management direction, such cuts tapered off in the 1980s and largely ended by the end of the decade. The evidence of this transition can be observed in the many stands of thirty to forty feet tall mixed coniferous forest that now covers most of the cut over lands of this watershed. The National Forest Management Act together with the Wilderness Act and Endangered Species Act made a large change in the manner in which the national forests are managed, but the change was borne from conflict between the Forest Service, the public and individual interest groups.

As a creation of the federal government the Forest Service must obey federal law. Yet, the entrenched leadership of the agency was not swept away by the new direction mandated by the National Forest Management Act, only its multiple use policy and the timber harvest biases built into the policy. The initial response of the agency was to swamp the public in sufficient paper documentation to discourage participation in the planning process. Interest groups like the timber industry with paid analysts would have the advantage in this arena. The first draft Flathead and Kootenai Forest Plans were complex documents with numerous and complex land classifications and management plans for each of those classifications. The approach underestimated the esteem in which the public held its public lands. Environmental, sportsmen's and other special interest groups along with those from the extractive industries took a keen interest in the process and became involved. The pattern was repeated across the west and the nation.

These groups brought to the process another dimension the Forest Service planners had not anticipated and industry hired analysts lacked. The local general public had collective intimate knowledge of the lands and resources of the forests. Several years earlier the Forest Service adopted a managerial scheme that transferred its upwardly mobile managers and experts on a roughly four-year basis. After a four year tour on a district or forest, the individual was transferred out to a new assignment. As a result, knowledge of the landscape was either lost or never accrued. Unlike the era of Roan Anderson when a ranger knew his district, managers and specialists were at a disadvantage to the local population who resided for many years in the area and knew their favored areas of the forests intimately. The new core of forest planners were, in many cases, hired to meet the requirements of the planning act and fresh to the Forest Service. The majority had nearly no first-hand knowledge of the lands for which they were drawing up plans. In those cases where the Forest Service personnel had local knowledge, it was still not a match for the collective knowledge of the interested public. The sportsmen's and environmental groups were adept at organizing the knowledge held by their constituents and focusing that knowledge on the forest planning process. Intended or not, Congress had leveled the playing field on how the forests were to be managed. In forest plan after forest plan, the public demanded that certain areas be protected and preserved in some manner. Most of these areas contained the remaining old growth forests on which forest harvest levels had previously been mortgaged. The result was inevitable. Timber harvest from the national forest lands declined dramatically as the initial round of plans were implemented in the 1980s and 1990s.

Additional laws and environmental pressures bore down on the prior timber harvest policy of the agency. The Endangered Species Act was passed prior to the National Forest Management Act, but its impact on forest harvest activities occurred in the 1990s as the status of rare, endangered and sensitive species became better known to the federal and state wildlife management agencies. The disappearance of salmon and steelhead runs in the forest streams of the Pacific Northwest was a major influence. The loss of cutthroat trout and other sensitive trout in the intermountain and Rocky Mountain west was a parallel and large influence. Specific impacts on wildlife were documented. The monoculture management of the forest for timber production limited the habitats and impaired streams with high sediments loads among other impacts. Species dependent on old growth were seriously affected. The spotted owl controversy of the Pacific Coast forests and woodland caribou issues in North Idaho are directly attributable to the loss of old growth habitat. As late as the early 1960s caribou were sighted in the vicinity of St. Maries Idaho, a hundred miles south of their now remnant range in the forest of the Selkirk Range north of Priest Lake. What the logging did not accomplish in habitat destruction, men dependent on logging accomplished with their guns.

None of this fit Roosevelt's legacy or the primary reasons the forests were reserved for all the people of America.

The National Environmental Policy Act required all federal agencies to develop environmental impact statements for any major action that might impact the environment. Lesser actions required environmental assessments, or at least some cursory level of environmental review. Public input was a requirement of all these review processes. In these activities as well the sportsmen's and environmental groups took full participation. Again there local knowledge of the land involved and all the resources the land harbored could not be ignored. The result of federal environmental laws, like forest planning, was to put on full display and allow full participation in the management of the public's lands. The days of decisions concerning those lands being made by a few line officers in relative obscurity were gone. The days when harvest of the forest to get the cut out could be pursued without question had ended.

The environmental and some sportsmen's groups recognized this fact. More important the forest planning and environmental policy acts gave these groups a recourse to oppose the continuance of the forest harvest policies. Decisions made by Forest Service Administrators could be appealed to the next higher level. Decisions made by rangers to forest supervisors and by forest supervisors to regional foresters were appealed. Some appeals went as far as the Chief of the agency. If not successful in altering the outcome, such appeals always delayed implementation and often changed aspects of the projects. The loss of time in the business world is nearly as crucial as the loss of the timber product, itself. Such tactics clearly made timber from the federal forest lands not only less plentiful, but also less reliable.

With forest plans in place and additional environmental law with which the agency was required to comply, projects could be challenged in a more neutral if not friendly arena, the court system. Planning a timber harvest project, especially in stands with little entry became nearly impossible without running afoul of parts of the forest plan or other required environmental law. Attempts to mitigate the impacts typically did not fully address the impact, but even so were a matter of interpretation by judges rather than resource specialists. Even in cases where Forest Service personnel attempted projects designed to address past mismanagement, it became nearly impossible to obtain a favorable outcome. A project in the Coeur d'Alene River's Little North Fork sought to decommission miles of roads built to support Idaho Jammer logging in the 1950s. The project would remove culverts and stream crossings directly attributable to water quality degradation. To monetarily support this needed environmental improvement, the district planners turned to some timber harvest. Some of the revenue from timber sales can be used to improve the area of the sale: K-V funds initialed for the Knutson-Vandenberg who authored the legislation. The environmental community did not oppose the water quality improvement work, but strictly opposed additional timber harvest in the already cut over Little North Fork watershed. The project was appealed and supported by the Forest Service administrators as necessary to meet water quality requirements dictated by the Clean Water Act. The environmental community argued that the timber harvest would cause additional sedimentation and hence violate water quality standards. After hearings in federal district court and the appellate court, the environmental community prevailed and no cut occurred. A few years later the project was recast with the water quality improvement work included, but all timber harvest excluded. Little objection to the project was forthcoming. The process on this single project from planning through the adverse decision absorbed roughly three-quarters of one Forest Service specialist's career.

Cases of fire damaged timber in roadless areas planned for salvage harvest were strongly opposed by those wishing to preserve the wild nature of those areas.

Areas of Oregon's Biscuit Fire were proposed for salvage unsuccessfully. Projects that involved any timber harvest were intensively planned by the Forest Service and as often intensively opposed by the environmental community. The inevitable outcome was a diminishment of the harvest from the federal forest lands and when timber was cut a reliable schedule was always in question due to appeals and protests.

The diminished emphasis on timber harvest wrought by implementation of the suite of environmental laws caused large changes in the forest landscape and the Forest Service itself. During the last decade of the twentieth century and first decade of the twenty-first, the forests began a recovery from the earlier cutting policy. Watersheds of North Idaho's Coeur d'Alene Forest were covered by large and visible clear cuts during the 1980s. Although forest regeneration was constant on the cool wet slopes of the Coeur d'Alene Mountains, the cutting pace maintained a constant and easily discerned inventory of recently cut over areas. As the cut diminished, the regeneration moved on apace. Most of the former cuts have regenerated into mixed coniferous forest with trees thirty to forty feet in height. The outlines of the former cuts are still perceptible to the trained eye, but the visual damage to the landscape is softening with every years' new growth. Areas remain, especially on north facing aspects, where shrub growth outstripped the tree growth. Tree growth and establishment as the dominant vegetation over the shrub layer is much slower on north slopes than on other slopes. These shrub fields persist and will for many years, in testament of the earlier harvest practices that failed to recognize the ecological sensitivity of these formerly forested slopes.

The diminished timber harvest and the realization that forest roads impact water quality adversely caused an analysis of the road systems in the forests. The Coeur d'Alene Forest was not only heavily cut, but, as a consequence, had a large road inventory. Analysis of these roads by Forest Service and state water quality specialists implicated these roads in the loss of pool habitat throughout the North Fork Coeur d'Alene River system including the majority of its tributary streams that experienced logging impacts. Without a need for these roads to remove timber, Forest Service specialists went to work decommissioning many of these roads. Initially entire road prisms were removed over the length of the road. However, analysis indicated drainage culverts, stream crossings, and those sections encroaching on the stream floodplains were the critical features requiring removal. The limited funding was focused on these areas in one sub-watershed after another throughout the river basin.

The work consumed nearly 15 years and goes on to date when funding can be found.

The beneficial impact on the river and its tributaries is evident. During the early 1990s the river and its tributaries were depleted of pool habitat required by trout. Cobble size sediment filled large sections of stream creating a preponderance of riffle and run stream structure. The constant loading of sediment from road failures and bank erosion maintained a stream system with far more sediment supply than stream power to effectively transport the sediment, especially the large particle fraction larger than gravel. The result was the bed deposition essentially filling most of the pools. As roads were decommissioned and the impacts removed, the sediment balance shifted during the first decade of the twenty-first century. The excess deposited sediment was exported and pool habitat reappeared along the river and in its tributaries. The habitat improvement linked with a catch and release rule instituted by the Idaho's Fish and Game Department has ushered in a renewed healthy cutthroat trout fishery. Such recovery is progressing throughout the forest.

There remain hangovers from the era of large timber harvests. The shrub fields generated especially on north facing aspects was mentioned. Logging in some drainages during the 1930s essentially high graded the forests. The desirable long lived seral species like western larch, white pine, and Ponderosa pine were harvested. More shade tolerant, less desirable and unfortunately more disease susceptible species, as white and Douglas fir and hemlock were left to dominate a majority of the mature forest stands. The eighty year suppression of all wildfires added to this tendency of the shade tolerant species predominating and away from dominance by the long lived seral species which predominate in stands subject to periodic low intensity fires. The result of over a hundred years of management errors in both timber harvest and fire suppression, is that most of the landscape of national forests are products of man's management decisions. Forest landscape patterns created by the environment and evolution converging to create a varied and more heterogeneous landscape are far less numerous. As a result some animal species continue to suffer habitat diminishment and degradation in opposition to the legacy Roosevelt intended.

Yet another positive change occurred during these same years that at least holds the promise of regaining National Forest true legacy. As the 1990s proceeded, many of the last of the Forest Service personnel that came up in the agency with the "get the cut out" ethic and whose performance was rated by this management direction, either reached retirement age or were discouraged by the application of environmental safeguards. To be sure a few of the old guard saw and embraced the change. A very few struggled daily to influence the leadership to alter the management. These few were on the vanguard of a new group of personnel that became the majority of journeymen professionals in the agency. These forest managers and specialists were better schooled in forest management and forest ecology as well as the many specialty sciences now necessary to manage the forests under the host of federal environmental mandates. These professionals were isolated by a generation from the "timber harvest above all other functions" ethic of their immediate predecessors. Although there were inevitable struggles between the old guard and the new managers and specialists, time and federal law favored the younger. The hydrologic, water quality, and road management of these new professionals recognized the impacts of the large road inventories and the effect on the water quality. These managers made the case for funding and found the means to remove roads making the difference evident today in the water quality and fisheries on the forests. These professionals had learned the value and necessity of fire in the forest ecosystems. Their influence put an end to an eighty year fire suppression policy that at best was loading the forest ecosystems for the next catastrophic burn like 1910, likely well before its scheduled reoccurrence. These professionals better understand the forest's ecology and dynamic structure. These professionals which have come to dominate the ranks of the agency are better equipped with the oversight of the public to guide the forests back from their unbalanced character to a more natural dynamic equilibrium. The Forest Service possess a core of professionals fully capable of guiding the national forests back to more balanced forest environments, balanced environments necessary to attain the legacy the forests were reserved to provide.

Agency Support: Forest Service Abandoned

Forest Service personnel accustomed to timber harvest levels of the 1950s through 1970s labored mightily to maintain the cut in the face of the National Forest Management Act and other key environmental laws. Initial efforts were made in the Forest Plan drafts which gave over large areas to timber management and retained language for other management areas that did not preclude timber harvest. Even areas without roads that were essentially rock and ice amongst the high peaks most often carried the caveat that timber could be harvested to combat insect infestations. Since there are always insects in the woods, the door was always open. These and other provisions designed to maintain the timber output were generally opposed by the majority of the engaged public. The general affect was a remarkable decrease in the proposed timber output by most forest plans. Since the plans were only a blueprint for forest management, the issues became basic on a project by project basis. Each project involved a federal decision affecting the environment and was thus subject to National Environmental Policy Act review and the strictures of other federal environmental law. Environmental and sportsman's groups opposed the projects that were perceived to harm their interests. In areas harvested heavily in the past where water quality and fishery impacts were apparent, most timber harvests at any significant scale were opposed. Sometimes upper Forest Service management revised downward timber harvests or at times, pulled back the proposed action. More often the cases went to federal court. Most often the timber harvest aspects of the project were found in violation of environmental law for one reason or another. The timber industry tried throughout the process to alter the outcomes, but the final arbitrator was now the courts and not the Forest Service officials or legislators.

During the 1990s federal forest land began to recover from the spate of timber harvests between the late 1940s and early 1980s. As noted elsewhere some areas will require many decades more to fully shake off the impacts of imprudent harvests. With the dramatic decrease in new harvests, and recovering old harvests, whole watersheds seemed to soften and green up during the twenty years after 1990. However the cost was a greatly reduced stream of timber from the federal forest. Try as the timber industry and the few remaining timber beasts in the Forest Service might, the forest plans, environmental law, and the engaged public no longer supported forest harvest. Demonstrations by timber laborers in the forest and the mills gained little notice and no outcry from the wider general public. Although dramatic procession of log trucks across the Nez Perce Road from Idaho to Darby Montana gained news coverage, the cause of loggers and log truck drivers did not capture much support from the general public on either side of the state line. Chambers of commerce in small towns and union workers in the mills complained, but the engaged public seldom responded, while the interest groups kept up tactics designed to foil any sale perceived as harmful. The general public either did not take sides or were disinterested unless a specific forest area dear to them was included in a project. In those cases, these individuals often joined the opposition, while a small but persistent group constantly favored all projects involving timber harvest. The same relatively small interest group continues its appeal for larger cuts in the current round of forest plans, but the excesses that benefited them in the past remain fresh in the minds of those who resist large timber harvests on the national forests.

As the cut declined from the federal forest the large timber companies turned to their private lands. The foresters overseeing these properties were most careful to ensure that harvest was controlled and renewable. The mill called for more timber, but at a point, it was not there to cut. Mills closed throughout the West. Areas like Coeur d'Alene and Post Falls that had seven or eight lumber mills had one by the early twenty-first century. The demand for lumber meanwhile did not diminish. Lumber streamed into the northern United States from across the Canadian border and from other counties worldwide. Timber interests sought to find timber to cut elsewhere and developed other sources. In Canada, where the provinces manage the "Crown Lands," many of the impacts to other forest resources that occurred south of the border, are in evidence in the timber stands north of the border. The impacts to wildlife like the Canadian lynx and woodland caribou are growing as dramatic as impacts to these species south of the border. In the United States domestic timber production remained a part of the equation from private and state lands with some federal timber input. However the demand gap was and currently is covered by timber harvested outside of the country's borders and not subject to the country's environmental laws. The costs may be higher, but this is passed along to the consumers along with the increased markup inherent to a higher cost.

With its timber supply issues covered, the timber industry no longer needed the agency or influence within the agency. Most of that influence embodied in the old guard timber beasts had retired by the late 1990s. Industry essentially withdrew its support in Congress for the agency. Congress has often been disproportionately influenced by the lobbyists working on behalf of industry, but after 1990, congress overwhelmingly became the captive of industry and the money behind its lobbying efforts. In times of forced austerity to pay for military adventures, entitlements, and runaway debt, the Forest Service with no lobbying support faced budget cutbacks that accelerated into the early twenty-first century and have now stabilized but at a low level of support. Recent budget sequestration by a bitterly divided Congress has only exacerbated the problem of adequately funding the management of our national forests. Ranger districts that had one or two staff dedicated to recreation only a few years ago, now have none with one individual charged with the recreation management responsibility for the entire forest. Forest specialists as hydrologists and fisheries biologists are not replaced. Enforcement of laws on the forests is limited to one or two individuals for millions of acres. The financial abandonment of the Forest Service and therefore, management of our national forests, is clear in the budget numbers.

What budget is left goes disproportionately to fire suppression. Firefighting priority is typically given for protection of homes and cabins built in the areas forest fires have naturally traversed for millennia. It might be argued that global climate warming has hastened the pace, but the avenues and terrains fires traverse are ancient, just not the homes and cabins foolishly placed in their path typically by wealthy and therefore politically powerful citizens. Politicians call for programs to abate the fire danger, typically through logging or forest thinning. Statements urging fire danger reduction were issued by Idaho's senatorial delegation at the height of the 2013 Beaver Complex fire that threatened Hailey and Ketchum. Yet as the pictures of the fire are examined the fuels burning are made up of a majority of grass and sagebrush with only dispersed groves of trees consumed as the fire reached them. Building fire defensible borders around homes and cabins may protect these structures, but logging would have little effect. Other than not building at all in locations prone to repeated fire events, defensible borders is the only viable solution. Yet logging is most always offered as the panacea to prevent the threat to private property.

Meanwhile right wing politicians in western states renew an old refrain to have the states manage the national forest. Most recently legislation sponsored by an Idaho representative to Congress forwards this proposition. Often the forests are represented as unhealthy and therefore fire prone due to bad federal management. State management is held out to do better. There are, of course, no real facts presented in a thirty second radio piece--only an illusion. That illusion can be dispelled quickly by the condition of blocks of state lands in places like Idaho's Floodwood or Priest Lake Forest. Here the tried and true clear cut methods that maximize timber output and hence dollars returned, demonstrate all the excesses of managing for one resource as the Forest Service did for thirty to forty years. Management of state lands in this manner follows the state constitutions. The constitutions of most western states require management the public lands for the maximum revenue mostly to support education. Would we expect any different interpretation for lands of our national forest given over to the states? Idaho has far fewer of the environmental safeguards analogous to federal law to protect the forest the timber interests covet. Certainly no facts are given to support the claim that forest fires are more prevalent on the federal estate as compared to that of the state. An inspection of annual fire maps suggests fire is indiscriminant in the lands burned over. What the state politicians fail to grasp is the simple fact that the national forest lands were set aside for all the people and to protect all values of the forests, not just their timber industry allies who still enjoy an inordinate amount of influence with state politicians.

Then there are the environmental groups. These groups are unfortunately firmly allied with the problem rather than the cure. Many still function as if it were twenty years ago with the Forest Service if not a sworn enemy at least not one they would consider aiding. Most have failed to recognize the two simple facts laid out here: the timber beasts and their management approach have been retired since the early 1990s and even if they were not, federal environmental law properly implemented and enforced by the courts will not permit a return to the management approach the timber beasts pursued. The Forest Service is an entity charged to protect large swaths of the environment, our national forests and given the task of managing these lands for all resources, including the founding vision of broad swaths of habitat for the large and mobile animals of the continent. If the environmental community is not firmly stuck twenty years in the past, why isn't the National Wildlife Federation, Ducks Unlimited, the Wilderness Society and Audubon Society not pounding on Congress' door to fund the Forest Service? These national environmental groups and several others banded together to attain significant environmental gains in the 2014 Farm Bill. Lobbying efforts of these groups tied farm subsidies and insurance offered by the federal government to wetland and native prairie protection. These conservation gains are laudable, but the scope of the habitat protected on private land is small compared to the habitat protected on our national forests. The difference might be that the national environmental organizations have a politically powerful group to partner with in the farm lobby, while the national forests, no longer geared to timber production, have little use to the politically powerful timber interests. One could argue that there is a politically powerful interest group associated with our national forests. These are the forest users who are a numerous and voting segment of the population. The environmental groups do not have a ready-made political ally in support of our national forests, but with education efforts these groups could create one. The environmental groups large and small could and should motivate the many forest users in support of good and reasoned management of our national forests.

None of this changes the fact that our national forests and the habitat they protect are under assault from vandalism and rampant unchecked motorized use. Why are not local environmental group pigeon holing every congressman visiting the home turf and asking why our national forest are not getting adequate support? Should the national debit be proffered as an explanation, it is easy to demonstrate on a local level, a greater fear of losing this unique treasured resource enjoyed by all the people to any attack by jihadists. Congressmen who do not agree, should be marked for replacement with representatives that do. It is high time for environmental groups, both national and local, to get active in funding our forests and parks ensuring the funding goes to activities that enhance all the forest resources, rather than a return to the logging sins of the past.

Strange Politics: National Forest Direction

The mission of the Forest Service drifted significantly after passage of the National Forest Management Act. Drift is an apt description for such a slow and sometimes meandering change that took nearly twenty-five years to achieve. The change remains a work in progress as Forest Service leaders, some political factions, and sympathetic politicians resist the will of the interested public that has hammered out the forest plans and their revisions. The shift from an emphasis on timber harvest and fire suppression to more balanced stewardship of the forest resources and the use of fire to assist forest management was slow. The shift caused pain to the employees of the agency, the public using the forest, and those economic interests that became dependent upon the federal timber supply. The change was gradual because it was in large part initially resisted by the old guard managers who were still in place as change began. These managers were supported by main street and timber industry interests that had grown dependent on the timber supply from federal land. Additional support came from local elected officials whose counties held significant acreages of federal forest lands and had lost the tax revenue from the economic impact of timber yielded from federal lands. The present day upswing of interest groups and their supporting politicians who advocate transfer of the national forests to state management is yet another misguided manifestation of a minority attempting to return the national forests to timber extraction as the primary management direction.

The result of Forest Plans directing less timber harvest and the immutable fact that the old growth timber was largely cut out and had not, as promised, been replaced by harvestable second growth, was a decline in local economies dependent on raw timber. Mills shut down and high paying jobs were lost. A national economy shifting away from resource extraction industry and towards more high technology and information management industries could easily adjust. However, local economies of cities and counties with large acreages of federal forest were harder hit. Since politics is in the end all local, elected politicians up to and including federal legislators especially in the West found it necessary to responds to protect their personal economic interests. The result was the Craig-Wyden legislation which made payments to rural counties with significant federal acreages in-lieu of taxes that presumably would have been created from economic activity on the federal lands.

Federal lands pay no property tax to the county. There were of course some tax revenues from goods (timber) and services created from the forest lands. However, most small rural counties rely almost exclusively on property tax to fund services. Economic activity on the forest lands only secondarily supported property tax revenue for the counties by supporting land owning tax paying citizens and business. In spite and possibly because the large federal tracts tied up in national forest paid no property tax, the Forest Service developed a policy of sharing the revenue from timber sales with the counties in which that timber was harvested. When timber harvest declined the funds shared declined. County budgets became dependent on this shared revenue in those counties of western states where large volumes of timber were harvested from federal lands. The Craig-Wyden payments were based on the idea that these payment should be maintained at least in part.

Yet the federal forest lands themselves require no county services. The county does not build or maintain the roads. There are no school children to educate living on the forest lands. There are no or at least should not be any indigent citizens requiring health care. They require no primary fire service. Some police service is required from the county sheriff, but only because the public goes out to use the forest lands. Presumably the public has paid for this service from its sheriff through the taxes paid on their private property. There is the issue of persons visiting from beyond the county borders to use the forest. The Coeur d'Alene River's North Fork and the St Joe River both located largely within the Idaho Panhandle National Forests have large summer use from the populace of Spokane area of eastern Washington who pay no tax to Benewah and Shoshone Counties of Idaho. However, these visitors bring their own economic stimulus in the form of recreational dollars spent in the county. Thus the federal forest lands require essentially no county revenue consuming services. The property tax reductions granted by most western states to private forest lands of greater than ten acres are based on these same presumptions as well. Yet the Craig-Wyden payments were made in lieu of timber sales revenues that have become limited and this revenue sharing has its historic roots in the replacement of property tax that might have been made from these federal lands, presumably if they were in private hands. The mathematics and logic of Craig-Wyden never added up, because timber sale revenue sharing in lieu of property tax for county services not required by the forest lands does not stand the test of logic. The program does make political sense for politicians at the federal level seeking to assist their constituents. Both Craig-Wyden and its predecessor timber receipts revenue sharing are a federal handout to counties with large acreages of federal lands. Yet only to those counties fortunate enough to have forest that supported large volumes of timber production.

A more reasoned justification for the legislation was to subsidize small rural counties for a time through the weaning of them from federal timber revenue sharing. A more cynical view might be that the payments subsidized the votes that kept powerful men in positions which create them great wealth. The same effect would likely have been created in these small counties if the budget had been supplied directly to the Forest Service to make improvements to the national forests. In some counties, local advisory boards did direct some of the Craig-Wyden funds to projects re-investing in the forests. However, such was not the case universally, nor was it professional forest managers making the decisions based on the forest plans, but rather a board easily swayed by backroom politics or county commissions responding to a local need. No matter, the use of these funds in the relatively few years they were available, federal budget restrictions soon made the payments a historical footnote. Notably much of their economic effect might be recaptured if the general public insisted that its federal government invest in the public's national forests. Such investments should mirror the forest plans worked out in consultation with the engaged public and be made by professional forest managers after the appropriate environmental review was completed. Perhaps this is a more positive remedy more consistent with the long term sustainability of the economies of counties dominated by federal forest lands than the short sighted fixes espoused by some elements of the rural west.

This alternate path is, of course, the often espoused idea of turning the federal forests over to state management. This simple change in administration would, in the minds of a vocal minority, solve the problems of the forests by placing them under the superior management of the states. The approach misses the obvious fact that these are national forests set aside for all the people of the nation not just those living on their borders or in the state of their location. An individual in Delaware has as much stake in the Flathead Forest as the resident of Whitefish, Montana which is flanked on three sides by the Flathead Forest. Although the Delaware resident has no expectation of a national forest in their state, they have the expectation of a national forest system where his stake is no more nor less than that of any other citizen of the nation. Many an eastern visitor to the West has stated that although they do not regularly use the western national forests, they take great solace that the forests exist and that those forests protect species and landscapes they will only experience in books, on-line, or on the Nature Channel. This view also ignores the overwhelming opinion of those inhabiting the towns and counties of the West situated close to the national forests. Many have chosen to live or come from families deep seated in these communities that see these forests as one, if not the main amenity, of their lives. Their ability to visit a forest, hike its trails, enjoy its streams, and ski or snow machine its hills is a prime motivation for remaining in these small towns. It is a prime motivation for settlement of many newcomers in numerous towns like LaGrande, Sandpoint, Whitefish and Baker City. The limits they place on expansion and the open space they provide is treasured. The protection they afford to the water quality and stability of the mountains is appreciated if seldom stated. The national forests are a major piece of the lifestyle of the vast majority of westerners.

The assumption that many who favor state management is that little would change on the forests, except of course that activities they favor would increase. Foremost among these are increased and more efficient timber harvest and unlimited access. Increased harvest is a given, because nearly all the constitutions of western states mandate the harvest of timber from state forest lands. This mandate would transfer to federal lands transferred to the states. Likely this is the prime reason that timber industry interests and the politicians they support favor state management. This state mandate would reduce the condition of the national forest to the cutover condition of the state forests which in notable cases is far worse than the worst abuses of the get- out-the-cut era of the past. A visit to Idaho's Floodwood Forest, tucked out of sight in the lower drainages of the Little North Fork Clearwater River, demonstrates the difference. The Floodwood Forest has been stripped of its timber to support the school system. As a thinly vailed piece of humor the Idaho's Land Board declared its namesake state park in the midst of the Floodwood. The park roughly twenty acres in size harbors a grove of large diameter red cedars spared from the chainsaw. The twenty acres is surrounded as far as the eye can see by clear cut forest. The Board went so far as to name the individual trees for its members who oversaw the cutting of the rest of the forest around the small twenty acre patch. Land Board State Park is a testament to the type of management our national forests would receive in the hands of state managers.

A comparison easier to view by the public is the forest management on any forested section 16 or 36 conferred to the state when granted statehood with nearby and often surrounding national forest lands. Even where the management of the national forest was driven for years by the timber production ethic of the mid to late twentieth century, the forest condition is superior on the federal forest. Transfer of the national forests of the West to state ownership is a prescription for transfer of these harmful practices onto our national forests. State management would constitute a return to abuses of the past which were repudiated by the

National Forest Management Act and replaced by forest planning in collaboration with interested forest users. It is a step backward from the improving conditions of the national forest landscapes.

The second issue with most advocates of state management is unlimited motorized access to the forests. Often this segment of the society sees motorized access as a right that has been restricted on federal forest lands. The right to visit and access federal forest is established. The mode of transportation is restricted however, to conserve the forests and their watersheds and wildlife. Often state forest has much greater access restrictions than federal forest. Most often roads developed to access and harvest timber are gated or in some other manner barriers installed after the harvest is complete on state forest land just as on federal forest land. Access for hunting is not encouraged on state forest land and has been restricted in certain cases. Groups championing transfer of federal forest to state management are unlikely to gain any additional access. Additional access will increase operation and maintenance costs and potentially harm timber growth. A state required constitutionally to produce revenue for schools has no interest in increasing its management costs or harming its timber crop. The expense of motorized or non-motorized trail systems and added road maintenance would only detract from school funding. Any state legislative attempt to alter the typical state management approach would not stand up to a constitutional test. Private timber companies operate in the same fashion as the state for identical reasons. Visit these private forest lands and the visitor will find restricted access to motorized vehicles is nearly universal. It is ironic that those demanding greater motorized access to national forests are likely getting the best possible access from a Forest Service mandated to consider all uses including access. Yet this vocal minority advocates a step that would eventually further limit their use of the forests.

More questionable is the use professional politicians make of the demands to transfer national forests to state management. The politicians claim that forest and fire management would be superior. Their clients, the forest industry, holds the view that federal forests are prone to fire due to poor management. These are of course, claims with no real data to show that fire is more prevalent on Forest Service managed land than on private or state forest. Since the ignition source of most fires in the west is lightning and lightning does not discriminate between land owners, it is unlikely that proportionally more or larger fires occur on the federal lands. If the private and state forests are as sustainable as advertised, then why the need for the federal forest to bolster the timber harvest? It is an easy matter to rebut the superior management of private forests. One needs only to look to the west from Coeur d'Alene Lake to Signal Point (Mica Peak). Completely owned by a private timber concern, the mountain appears threadbare from the constant timber harvest. A long-time resident of the area stated the case best by declaring that one could discern easily where the ski area on Signal Point was once located. It is the only area with a continuous cover of trees, only because the trees are too young to harvest.

Forest industry propagandists often liken the forest to a garden or the row crops of a farm. Managing a forest is reduced to the simple matter of harvesting and replanting, which is in essence tree farming. There is nothing wrong with such management on private lands or even state lands dedicated constitutionally to timber production. However, this is not the sole or even the primary purpose of our national forests. These lands were withdrawn to maintain forests which are known to science as far more complex and biologically rich assemblages of plants and animals than tree farms. Far too much of the federal forests became tree farms during the latter half of the past century. Our national forests are moving away from their dark past when timber production and mere tree farming were the primary management direction on the national forests. Through forest planning mandated by the National Forest Management Act, the interested and engaged publics helps steer the direction for its forests. Having lost the planning battles to the will of most engaged participants, the timber industry and the politicians that serve them attempt a new tactic of making the forest state domain on the lame promise that forests will be better managed.

The timber industry's interests intersect with those who see the federal lands as their own personal domain, failing to recognize the equal stake all citizens have in these lands. Those supporting transfer to the states to increase their motorized access or to increase timber production to bolster local economies fail to gage the state and private industries track record. Both the state and private forest land tend to exclude motorized access. Timber harvest on private land is typically pursued to the point that the forest pantry is bare resulting in mill shutdowns. This is a story told a hundred fold over across the West in town after town, whether dependent on private, state or federal timber sources. Forest are overcut to meet demand. In the case of the federal forests the rotational period to produce harvestable second growth is deflated to increase the cut. All look the other way until of course the natural system, operating on its own time tables little influenced by man's efforts, has been used up. Mills close and the boom bust cycle is perpetuated. Operating a private business in this manner is a matter for the shareholders to decide. Operating the state forests in this manner is a question ultimately for the voters to approve. Operating the national forests in this manner has been precluded by federal law, which is fully supported by most national forest stakeholders who hold these forests as not only special but also endowed to the American public as far more than just a timber source. Since the 1940s the timber industry has sought, in one manner or another, to change the wider use perception of our national forests as guardians and producers of many resources. Industry was successful for a time until the public awoke to the consequences in the 1960s. The law was changed at the federal level in the mid-1970s. Industry now was forced to compete with the many other forest users. Industry did not prevail in the forest planning battles nor could timber harvest projects often meet the strictures of other federal environmental laws. The latest ploy to place the national forests under state management is just another attempt to make timber harvest the primary management objective of the national forests. The national forests have a higher purpose than additional ground for tree farmers. The public who use and admire these forests know the high purpose instinctively whenever they see or enter their national forests. An alerted public will again send the timber industry packing back to its own lands. On the state lands that same public may wish to examine the excesses that occur in the name of funding the schools statewide.

The difference was so eloquently placed in the words of his character Ranger Bill Bell by Montana author Norman Maclean. Known for his strict conservation of words, Bill Bell draws the difference as "Men that love the woods without thinking they own them." Timber interests demanding a large harvest, those demanding more motorized access over the requirements of other resources and values, and even the rich who block access to the national forest with their own private land are seeking to own the woods in part by not sharing equally with all the other users, values and resources. The National Forest Management Act supported by federal environmental law is the keystone body of legislation on how these differences should be worked out among resources and users. Since these forests belong to all of the country's citizens, they are and should remain national forests. Those few words placed for Bill Bell to express should be a test of any idea or motive for managing our forests should be applied.

Some Remedies

When problems and issues are perceived by a large part of the general public, solutions are quickly found. This is the general track record of the American democratic process. The politics of minority favoritism and special interest deals collapse under the glare of general public awareness and the public's innate sense of fair play. The unfortunate fact of the politics of the initial decades of the twenty first century is an apathetic, often confused, and certainly unled but centrist public, buffeted between the extremes of the left and the right. The core solution to a
Forest Service lost from its core mission is the solution necessary to solve many of the nation's problems. A great many ideologues and special interest representatives in Congress need to be discarded and replaced with individuals who solve the problems of the general public and with the ability to negotiate with others of differing opinions to refine and improve those solutions. The centrist majority that makes up the core of this country must reclaim power from the current core of our representatives that put themselves above their constituents to line their pockets and represent special interests that they have cynically convinced themselves are the interests of their constituents or worse, from the ideologues who represent the ideas of the few rather than the majority.

Unfortunately the lack of solution to many of the Forest Service's issues are bound up in the current general malaise of our political system. However, there is a solution. The solution is a general public that knows what it wants and expresses those desires in the many media available and most importantly at the ballot box. The core of the problem is a centrist majority that is not fully engaged because it is not inspired. Perhaps our national forests are a treasure so great that the public can and will come together over their protection and management. However, synthesis of political will takes leadership. Currently that leadership is sorely lacking. A Teddy Roosevelt, capable of perceiving, communicating, and embodying the national will is needed.

The natural leaders of any public movement on behalf of our forests and the agency charged with their protection are those environmental activist groups that are the inheritors of Roosevelt, Muir, Grinnell, Pinchot, Mather, and Marshall. Among these forefathers of the environmental movement, there existed difference in philosophy, but the body of their work in national parks, wildlife refuges, forests and wilderness, is on the landscape of the country. These men did not allow differences to obscure the overall objective.

Unfortunately, their environmental inheritors have. Many national and certainly most grass roots local environmental groups retain a lack of trust in the agency charged to protect the national forests. The suspicion is well founded in the errors in Forest Service management during the central years of the twentieth century. Environmental groups are well advised to keep a watchful eye on the agency, but currently this is so often practiced with sufficient animosity that no support of the agency is forthcoming. It is just this lack of support that causes insufficient budgets. Limited budgets equate into limiting agency staffing, limited management and limited enforcement of the regulations on our national forests. At best, the public is unconcerned with these forest resources and only with their personal pursuits which in many cases are left to run wild over our forests. The illegal ATV paths, dumping, and watershed damage are testimony on the ground to these results of insufficient funding. At worse are the claims that the state forest management agencies could do better at management of our national forests. This proposition was revealed as faulty earlier in this text based simply on the constitutional mandate of most state forest management agencies.

The clear solution to the underfunding issue is for the environmental groups of all stripes to make sufficient funding of our national forests a first priority. It matters little whether a group has national, state or local support or whether it supports wildlife habitat conservation, wilderness designation, outdoor recreation, field sports or for that matter reasonable harvest of timber, the canvas upon which all these interests and pursuits can be sketched is the national forests. These forests must be maintained, nurtured and improved to achieve any one group's goals. All groups with an interest in our national forests must join a campaign for the proper funding of the agency charged with the protection of these forests. The track record is that environmental groups are dedicated to preservation of the land and water. For good reason that dedication has led to a healthy questioning of all land and environmental management arms of government. Yet, if carried to the extreme that many groups practice today, it is harmful to the resources the groups seek to protect. Environmental groups need to push hard politically for better funding of the Forest Service. Support of adequate funding is hardly mutually exclusive from cautious and diligent oversight of the agency.

Environmental groups are only the seed around which the political will of the nation must be gathered and directed. The general public is supportive of its national forest. Creating this realization among the general public is not a difficult task. The environmental groups have a superior and far less abstract product to sell. The public use and admiration of its forests has been clearly and repeatedly demonstrated. Volunteers groups made up of hikers, backcountry horsemen, cross country skiers, snowmobilers and trail bikers donate many thousands of person-days work to maintain forest resources. These dedicated groups are a natural allies in any campaign for additional funding. Any additional federal investment in these forests is an investment directly in the economies local to them. Local Chambers of Commerce should lend support for this reason alone. Those political forces peddling fear of foreign powers of terrorist groups are able to sell the general public on the need for large defense budgets. These political forces are successful even though the chance of actual physical harm to the vast majority of Middle Americans is remote. As with the forest it is not argued that we not be vigilant as a society, but such vigilance should be applied to the size of the budget spent. A simple case can be made over the western section of the country that the national forests add more to the quality of life than any threat of jihadists detracts. A similar case can be made around the eastern forests. In the urban centers that are often the political tail wagging the dog, the pure vision of a place far from the crowded urban existence where nature rather than man dominates has been and remains a powerful spiritual elixir. The vision was powerful for urban dwellers like Grinnell and Roosevelt in the late nineteenth century and it remains as powerful in the far more urbanized America of the twenty-first century. The environmental groups have a case to make. The environmental and sportsmen's groups have a campaign to pursue. The campaign is winnable. Congressmen, no matter what their party or ideology will bow to the will of a determined and informed public. It is up to the environmental and sportsmen's groups to set aside their difference with the Forest Service to lead this campaign.

When additional and stable funding is obtained, the issue will arise concerning its expenditure. Such battles will certainly be joined just as soon as it is apparent the political will has been amassed to support funding increases. The direction of these funds will be most important to the health of our forests and the subsequent support of the general public. Given the current under manning of the agency, some budget will be required to bolster personnel. Enforcement capabilities should be a highest priority. All the travel and management plans have little use unless the manpower is available to see they are followed. However, the real need in the national forest is for reinvestment.

The national forests require reinvestment in their infrastructure. Many forest road require improvement and in cases, relocation to limit erosion and subsequent sedimentation of streams. A good many road should be either banked or decommissioned, removing them from use. Those roads retained in the travel plan to provide adequate access should be upgraded significantly. Trails should be another emphasis for funding. Many trails have been allowed to deteriorate to a point that these are unusable. There are cases where hiking trails prominently featured in hiking guides thirty years old are now so deteriorated that traversing these trails is impossible for the average hiker. Some skilled hikers practice "trail archeology" to find these routes faint trace through the forest. An inventory of all trails, extant and historic should be developed on each forest. A public process should be developed to define both the motorized and non-motorized trails. The travel planning process on many forests completed this process in part, yet the plan failed to address those historic trails that budgetary constraints had long since allowed to disintegrate. Such trails might not be desired by the public. However, in North Idaho, there are significant sections of the Idaho Centennial Trail that are mapped on paper, but when one attempts to traverse these it is found the trail has long since gone to ground as the result of neglect. In other cases, encroachment of private land development has blocked access trails into the forests. New access over routes secure from the encroachment of development are required. Motorized trails for both single track and all-terrain vehicles use has burgeoned in the past thirty years. Trails to accommodate these uses require construction in some cases but more often existing trails require relocation away from sensitive resources and fortification especially at stream crossings to resist the erosion wheeled use can engender.

Additional reinvestment is required in forest facilities and the forest itself. Campground and recreational areas require constant upgrade. During high use periods these facilities require more patrolling and policing than camp hosts can provide. At very least sufficient Forest Service enforcement personnel should be on call and close enough to make a difference. The season that campground facilities are available should be extended into the heart of western hunting seasons. As a result of personnel shortages campgrounds are closed during this second peak in forest use. Closing campgrounds forces hunters into camps that are less desirable but, more importantly, often are more damaging to the forest environment. Often large numbers of hunting camps with no sanitary facilities are located quite close to trailheads and water bodies. Campgrounds are sited and provided facilities to absorb the impact of many users, while the places hunters are forced to camp often do not meet these criteria and certainly do not have the protective facilities. The unfortunate track record is that due to budget constraints and another factor, the migration of the Forest Service to town, the manpower is not available to police the recreational facilities and to keep them in operation when they are required to protect the forest. When once Forest Service personnel were located year around just across the Redfeather Area's Dowdy Lake from the popular campground, now only a visitors' center is maintained between the Memorial and Labor Day holidays.

Re-investment is needed in our forest's timber stands and their management. Management should not be for timber values alone. Rather forest stands should be managed to maximize values as old growth, diversity, wildlife habitat, timber production, recreational aesthetics and watershed protection. The cutover areas unrecovered to forest should be managed to re-establish growing stands. Those land formerly cut over that have re-established forest cover should be inventoried and assessed. Revised forest plans should set criteria and conditions that guide the maturation of these stands to supply the range of forest values. Certainly, timber harvest would be one of those values, but management of a stand for harvest should follow objective criteria based on forest culture, not the needs of industry or the local economy. Objective criteria should also govern the management of forest stands for old growth, wildlife habitat or any of the other values. Such management of stands is already possible through computer based geographic information systems that not only record the boundaries, management history and physical characters of individual stands, but can also be used to model management outcomes before any additional management actions are taken. Forest management plans of the future would better serve the public if they focused on smaller areas of the forest, possibly the ranger district or large watershed.   A two year planning process would seek to achieve a balanced management of forest culture for all the values the public desired. As many specific projects that could be foreseen should be incorporated into the plan. After such a planning process was completed with participation and consensus by all interests, the environmental impact assessed and the decisions necessary made, it would not be necessary to revisit the planning in the smaller area for another fifteen to twenty years as the National Forest Management Act requires. Planning and plan implementation based on smaller logical units than the entire national forest and use of advanced geographic information systems modeling of management scenarios could provide the Forest Service and the public a better route to managing the national forests for the desired forest values with less subsequent conflict.

Timber harvest has a place in the proper use of the national forests. Selective cutting or small opening group selection can assist the opening of stands and the creation of small openings advantageous to wildlife. On lands where timber grows quickly and harvested stands can be re-established in a reasonable ten to fifteen years with young healthy trees, timber harvest is an appropriate activity on the national forest lands as long as other resources are not unduly compromised. In the Pacific Northwest, successful harvest strategies involve small areas of ten to fifteen acres, where many but not all of the dominant trees are harvested and a large number of wind firm seed trees are left have a good record of restoring young growing timber stands in reasonably short periods, while still retaining much of the forest character. The seed tree to heavy seed tree-shelter wood harvest systems may require an additional entry in fifteen to twenty years to remove the over-story initially left behind, but in many locations, these better mirror the natural forest regeneration and succession than wholesale clear cuts, which often leave harsh environments for tree establishment. Such cutting can be designed to encourage wildlife. Cutting systems that best hasten forest re-establishment are typically unique to the forest type and its environment. Other harvest approaches may be more appropriate elsewhere in the National Forest System that covers a broad range of environments. A hundred years of forest management indicates to forestry professionals and the public, those systems best suited to a specific area. Those are the systems that should be applied with the primary goal of forest culture to enhance the forest environment for all resources, not timber harvest for the local economy or industry support. Timber management with a goal of forest culture coupled with fire management approaches ranging from controlled burns to letting fire burn naturally on the landscape will over time attain a land management vision worthy of our forests.

Often those bent on cutting the forest argue that the clear cut mimics the stand replacement fire. Ecological studies, especially those completed in Oregon, indicate that the similarity is superficial at best. In addition in an era of warming temperatures and drying forests in the West, there is little need to mimic the stand replacement fire in the national forests or elsewhere on the landscape. Much of the western landscape is and will be in recovery from such fires for many decades.

The national forest lands should be managed for all the resources these support and for the dependency of those resources on adjacent lands. Too often the forests lands are thought of by their managers as islands somehow cut off from adjacent property. The activities contemplated for national forest lands are somehow unrelated to those implemented just across a border. The fact is that many resources, including wildlife, water and air freely and easily cross these borders. Some regulations may govern uses on the adjacent property, but the management of that property is the sole prerogative of the owner. If the national forests are viewed as a reservoir of conserved forest lands then the management of these forests must be, in part, shaped by what has occurred near their borders.

An example was an initiative by a district of the Idaho Panhandle National Forests to restore stands in a watershed with a history of high grading timber and of considerable mining. Set in a management philosophy of encouraging the long lived seral species such as larch, white, and Ponderosa pine a number of burns and timber harvests were proposed. In addition, erosion and sedimentation problems were to be addressed by road and culvert removal. The road and culvert removal make a contribution to the sedimentation problems in the stream, but that contribution would be small. Adjacent private land harbors a mine site that contributed massive quantities of sediment as compared to the quantities coming from forest lands. A better approach to control sediment impacts may have been to file suit under the Clean Water Act against the responsible mining company seeking actions to abate the erosion from the mined property. Work on the federal lands would then have some additional beneficial impact. In a similar manner, the timber stand work ignored the fact that the adjacent drainage to the south was largely in private timber company ownership and had been severely clear cut harvested during the past twenty years. Area wide, young fast growing forest with the long lived seral species sought would not be in short supply in the general area for many years to come. It can be argued that the controlled burning and timber harvest proposed would potentially improve the stands on national forest lands, an admirable objective. However, such improvements should not be argued on their own merit without a broader scale view of the local landscape. Part of national forest management should involve buffering the resources that exist on them against management decisions made adjacent to them. Managed with this broader view, the national forests will achieve the original design as reservoirs of the land's vital resources. A second benefit might also be accrued. State and private land mangers might alter or be encouraged to alter their own timber management styles, if it is apparent that the practice ultimately limits timber harvest on the federal estate. If this norm were established, the national forest would be extending their influence on the wise management of all the nation's forest resources.

Re-investment in our wilderness areas is another pressing need. Currently trail systems in many wilderness areas are being lost. Hunting outfitters, hunting groups or Backcountry Horsemen currently complete most trail maintenance in the wilderness. Wilderness trails require special treatment, because the mechanized equipment necessary to more quickly clear and maintain trails is prohibited by the Wilderness Act. The designation and special management should not be a detriment to accessing of these areas. The wilderness trail systems require significant re-investment so these crown jewels of our national forest lands are accessible to those willing to shed the mechanized amenities and return to simpler means of travel and camping. The heritage and history of our land lives in these special lands. The heritage is available to all who seek it out.

The old fire lookouts are another area requiring re-investment. The relicts of a simpler time and lifestyle dot the high peaks of our national forest lands. Many are falling into disrepair at a time when the remaining fire lookouts are rented to the public for short stays. The Forest Service should be investing in the remaining viable fire lookouts and replacing some lost as recreational facilities. The inspirational views that almost every fire lookout command are a resource that will only increase in demand from the public. It should not be left to dedicated private individuals to maintain and preserve these national treasures that are akin to the lighthouses of our shores.. Funds should be allocated to reinvest in fire lookouts as recreational treasures.

The greatest re-investment required is manpower. The manpower required is those individuals working on the ground in the national forests. Currently two Forest Service law enforcement officers are on duty for the Coeur d'Alene River Ranger District of the Idaho Panhandle National Forest. The District makes up the entire Coeur d'Alene National Forest which is only administratively managed as the part of the Idaho Panhandle National Forests. Two trained enforcement officers and a couple of other staff with some enforcement authority are assigned to cover the 1,135 square miles of the forest with thousands of miles of roads and trails. The pattern is repeated throughout the disciplines required to adequately manage the Forests. Typically one individual for recreation, roads, timber management, or fire. Often for the specialties as fisheries biologists, wildlife biologists or hydrologists only one individual has the work load for the entire national forest. The Forest Service has responded to smaller budgets with cuts in any operations largest cost: the work force. As a result the work force managing our national forests and responding to the demands of the public and illegal activity on the forests is threadbare. Unlike the National Park Service that collects an entrance fee as well as camping fees, many of the uses of the national forest come without any charge. Yet the forests are generally more easily accessed over a larger area while access in the National Parks is focused. The Forest Service has instituted some minor users' fees and has captured the assistance of volunteer groups. However the fees are often evaded due to limited manpower and the volunteer hours are insufficient to properly address the task of managing our national forests. The only path to proper management of our forests is re-investment in them including re-investment in an adequate staff to manage these national treasures.

Much the re-investment work required by our forests will require just that: hard work. Building road and trails, rebuilding facilities in campgrounds and lookouts, planting trees, thinning and brushing. Existing contractors likely could not handle the work load built up through years of neglect. Adequate work force for many of the re-investment projects required by our forest could be patterned after the depression era approach championed by FDR. A new Civilian Conservation Corp could be organized through participating states. The state could more efficiently couple the unemployed or chronically out of work populace with work projects on the forests. At best unemployment rates sit nationally chronically at five percent, while many rural counties of states far exceed this threshold. The federal government, states with forest and their counties could find ways to employ the unemployed and tie welfare payments to real work improving our forests. The work would not be high technology or an automatic entry into a career ladder, but it would instill a work requirement on the able yet chronically non-employed of the nation. If properly administered, it would create an alternative to crime and chronic non-employment while supplying the additional work force needed to make substantive improvements in our forests. A management cadre would be necessary to direct the work force, allowing for some advancement opportunity into the management structures of the state and Forest Service. Many Forest Service employees of the fifties, sixties and seventies started as CCC employees in the thirties and came back to Forest Service employment after the war. A similar opportunity might be afforded those capable but currently chronically unemployed.

A call to spend more money on a domestic program or any program seems counter to the national interest in times of deficit federal spending. Yet that argument can be countered by a simple reply. As a taxpaying citizen, what am I getting back from my federal government that enriches my life? The federal government spends heavily servicing a national debit, entitlements, and defense including foreign aid with domestic programs a small fraction of the remaining expenditures. Debt service and entitlements are burdens imposed by fiscal irresponsibility practiced over decades. These burdens could be addressed in part, but these are subjects more complex and not directly germane to the future of the Forest Service or the question posed earlier in the paragraph. Defense, including foreign aid, is however a different matter. Certainly it is the duty of the federal government to protect the country. Unfortunately that mandate has been used and abused to funnel federal funding to contractors tied to the defense establishment. Several undeclared war actions have produced questionable tangible results in defense of the country while defense contractors profit. Foreign aid appears a lofty action, but an analysis of foreign aid typically finds a special interest within this country profiting most. The culture of congressional catering to special interests and the contributions of those interests back to the congressional benefactors is so blatant that little effort is made to conceal the inside relationship. At the same time public support of congressional performance is in the single digits. An average middle class wage earner contributes between forty-five to fifty-five hundred dollars in taxes to the federal government. When that individual asks what those funds purchase for them personally, little can be found. A separate gasoline tax covers the federal highways they use. A secure country is appreciated but could be secured with better protection of the borders and less attempts to address threats half way around the world on ground that is difficult to hold and secure over time. The entitlement programs, social security and Medicare being the largest, are paid into, but the question of any return from a fiscal pyramid scheme haunts those who think about the odds as population growth diminishes. Viewed from down on the ground, the average citizen is forced to answer that little is returned to them from the federal taxes paid. The domestic discretionary spending left to the federal government is typically diverted to those who contribute a portion back to the congressmen who nurture the special interest political system.

The federal taxpayer and especially those concerned with the quality of our life must put their foot down on the neck of Congress. The message from the voting public should be a theme of re-investment. Re-investment in our public infrastructure. Re-investment in our national parks, monuments, and forests. Re-investment in those amenities that nurture the public soul of Middle America. The government must re-invest in a manner that strengthens and broadens the middle class rather than steer funds to those industries that enrich the few at the expense of the many. The ultimate power to enact this change in course lays squarely in the hands of an aroused and vigilant electorate. The power lies in the middle with the moderate who is largely ignored by the radical wings that appear to sway the two political parties. A leader must arise from the middle. A leader and group around that leader with clear vision that builds the middle class of the country and those institutions that nurture the soul of the middle class. Among those institutions are our national forests where so many resort to touch the inspiration of the natural world.

Re-investment will require a change in the political will of the electorate, but the Forest Service as an agency might lead the way to change by example. Changes in its current culture would in themselves move a long way to improvement of our national forests. These changes may be forced by political change but they could be instead managed by the Forest Service leadership examining its earlier successes in land management and how these were achieved. The Forest Service cannot go back to those simpler days, but it can gain lessons from those days and adapt these to today's realities and superior science and technology. The result will have a better chance of improved management of our forests than the current pattern of neglect.

The primary lesson from the past is a thorough knowledge of the land. Rangers like Ed Pulaski and their inheritors like Roan Andersen knew the land that they managed. These men had walked the ground and had a firm knowledge of its resources and limitations. These men spent considerable time on the land they managed both in terms of work days and career time. They were out on the ground inspecting the crews' work and the land they were expected to manage. When the need arose they could make correct and accurate management decisions based on their knowledge of the land. By contrast the ranger of the current Forest Service spends a minimum amount of their time out on the district and typically has a short tenure on that district. The staff supporting the ranger typically spends more time on the ground, but any advancement in the agency of today requires the individual to change jobs and districts or forest roughly every four years. Hence the agency continually casts off its institutional knowledge of the lands it manages. There are exceptions and exceptional individuals who buck the tide by remaining on a forest or district through the majority of their career, but these individuals pay the price of no or minimal advancement in the agency. The days when an Emil Grandjean might advance from seasonal help to forest supervisor without leaving the same forest are currently gone from the Forest Service. The cynical euphemism holds that any advancement to line officer is through the chief's office in Washington, where the green shorts of agency correctness are issued. Yet office hours provide little knowledge or wisdom of the national forest lands to be managed. The land not the office and agency culture should be the priority concern.

Many line officers of the agency steeped in the culture of rapid staff turnover argue that computerized geological information systems can record for all the resources on the ground where these can be read by anyone in the comfort of the office. They will argue that rapid staff turnover limits the development of cozy relationships with public served; euphemized in the language of the agency as "going native." Yet computerized systems only create a reflection of reality, not reality itself. Any knowledgeable computer or imagery analyst will constantly emphasize the necessity to ground truth all information. Cozy or preferential relationships can be managed with a culture of strict ethics. This approach is preferable to constant turnover that sacrifices institutional knowledge of the land. The track record is that the turnover management strategy did nothing to alter preferential relationships that developed well up in the hierarchy of the agency in the past. A prime upper management responsibility is to guard against preferential treatment through the ranks not to foster it.

If the Forest Service returned to the basic approach of its personnel knowing and understanding the landscape it managed, the result would be superior management and care of the national forests. Line officers and the technical specialists who support knowledgeable management would be afforded the time necessary to fully appreciate the landscape upon which their decision will have effects--not just the physical landscape but the political and social landscape affected by the decisions. Time would be afforded to know the public that they served and know the public's desired forest values. Too often the federal managers are viewed as passing through the community in which they temporarily reside for a short period. All too often the decisions and relations are arrived at by a substantial community effort, only to be vacated or misinterpreted by the next cadre of managers to move into the next roughly four year stint. In one case a volunteer group managing a cross country ski area worked with the local ranger district to develop a cost share agreement with the Forest Service. A year after the agreement was signed a new ranger took over management of the district. The new ranger began to challenge points covered in the agreement without as much as bothering to read the agreement. The result of such management miscues is eventual mistrust by the communities with which the Forest Service should be working. A longer tenure in an area will minimize misunderstandings. Forest Service personnel will know and understand the national forest's neighbors becoming trusted members of the community. Under these situations decisions can be made that are positive for the forest yet detrimental to some local interest. The affected party may not appreciate the decision, but can still respect his neighbor who made the adverse decision. The current personnel management scheme based on rapid turnover creates a local versus federal employee division that only creates mistrust and an adversarial relationship. There is a reason old style rangers were revered and often their names, together with a good deal of their career achievements, are remembered in the communities in which they lived and worked. These men were a trusted part of the community over a long period. They were etched in the fabric of the community. The four year and on to the next assignment personnel management approach in use by the Forest Service since the 1970s is simply too short a time to build lasting relationships of trust. The upper management of the Forest Service should seriously examine it personnel policies with a view to extending tenure in key positions while allowing for career advancement as well.

Sum Up

Theodore Roosevelt's master environmental stroke was the preservation of a broad system of national forests. The system created protected the broad swaths of habitat necessary to maintain the large mammals of the mid latitudes of North America. In the process habitats for any number of plants and animals were protected. In addition a legacy treasured by the vast majority of Americans was created. The legacy exists because a few far sighted individuals acted decisively and effectively while the majority interest group at the time was politically outmaneuvered. The subsequent generations of all Americans from that time to this have ratified the far sighted wisdom of the few over the greed of the few. To this day environmentally concerned citizens fight the battles necessary to maintain the legacy of our national forests.

The Forest Service was charged by the government to manage these lands. During its earliest history, two ecological flaws were imbedded in the Forest Service's management of the forests. One was a nearly blind belief for nearly a hundred years in the European model of forest management introduced by the founding chief and some early employees of the service. The second was a blind prejudice against all fire in the forests engendered by the bitter experience of 1910. These two inherent flaws were capitalized on by a cadre of forest managers who concentrated disproportionately on the production of timber from the national forests most often to the jeopardy of other valued resources. A period of excessive unstainable timber harvests ensued from the 1950s through the 1970s. As resource limitations on the national forest became more and more apparent during the 1960s and 1970s the general public that greatly values its forests revolted and expressed through Congress its will to be included in the forest planning process. The National Forest Management Act is the legal embodiment of that desire. Despite efforts of the Forest Service to cloak the process in a blizzard of paperwork, a dedicated public persevered and, in actual fact, proved to be more knowledgeable of the resources of the forests than the service authorized to protect and manage them. The resulting forest plans greatly reduced the proposed cuts from the national forests. As the plans, which are mere management blueprints, were implemented in projects, the concerned public remained engaged and drove the accountability of the Forest Service to the large body of federal environmental law enacted in the late 1960s and 1970s. The result has been decreased timber harvest on the national forest and an opportunity through other actions and time to heal some scars created by the era of heavy timber harvest.

As the initial battles over forest plans and post plan projects played out, most of the Forest Service personnel associated with the period of heavy cuts retired and were replaced by more balanced managers. In addition, a cadre of technical specialists better equipped to address the environmental issues created by past harvests was hired and implemented a respectable amount of remedial work. However, none of this work restored the timber harvest from the national forests that the timber industry desired. After its failure to increase the timber cut, the industry tapped timber resources outside the country where environmental safeguards either are less restrictive or do not exist. Since the industry no longer gained from the national forest and the Forest Service, it withdrew its support of budgets in Congress. The Forest Service today teeters forward underfunded and undermanned.

The environmental and some sportsmen's groups continue to oppose the Forest Service on most issues and do little to assure that the appointed guardian agency of our national forests is adequately funded. Meanwhile our forest are degraded not by timber sales but by rampant illegal ORV use, vandalism, and numerous other illegal activities. The Forest Service has little ability to police the forests given the budget restraints. Damage the timber beast created is healing just in time for a second wave of damage from an uncontrolled public. While environmental and other interest groups argue over the next round of forest and travel plans, the great unspoken and largely unrecognized specter in the room is that such plans are meaningless unless personnel and budget are available to implement and enforce the plans. The environmental and sportsmen's groups that have the largest stake in maintenance of the national forests play into the hands of the conservative politicians and their timber industry allies who would place large sections of the forests under state control and renewed management with timber harvest the prime goal.

Groups supportive of the national forests and the proper management of those forests for all their values, including habitat preservation and maintenance of natural environments, must begin a campaign in support of funding the Forest Service. The general public whether they be hikers, horsemen, trail riders, hunters, berry pickers or a family out to camp or picnic support and greatly appreciate the legacy and the experiences the national forests add to our lives. These natural constituents of the forests can be mobilized to inform Congress that the current funding situation of our natural resources in general and our forests specifically is unacceptable. Otherwise the federal government will spend the funds on foreign wars and military hardware that largely put those dollars in the pockets of the large corporate allies who support them with donations. If placed in the glaring light of public opinion, most Americans would choose proper funding of their national forests and the agency charged with managing them, over foreign aid to many of the countries that receive that aid. The problems is that the general public is not informed. The public is not informed because the environmental and sportsmen's groups have failed to make this issue important to the public. These groups are mired over twenty years in the past fighting a Forest Service that no longer exists as it did in 1990. Those among us who cherish and value national forests for what they are and can be must promote protections of the natural habitats of the mid latitudes of the continent and put the past behind us and push for funding of our forests. We must be ever vigilant that those forests are managed in a balanced manner to maximize all their resources. We must remain true to Teddy Roosevelt's vision and legacy by influencing and shaping the agency that manages our national forests.

REFERENCES

1. Brinkley, D. G. 2009 *Wilderness Warrior: Theodore Roosevelt and the Crusade for America* HarperCollins New York. 960 p.
2. Goodwin, D.K. 2013 *The Bully Pulpit* Simon and Schuster New York 910 p.
3. Morris, E. 2010 *Colonel Roosevelt* Random House New York. 766p.
4. Millard, C. 2005 *The River of Doubt* Doubleday New York. 416p.
5. Luoma, J.R. 1999 *The Hidden Forest* Henry Holt and Company New York. 228p.

ACKNOWLEDGEMENTS

Appreciation for much of the substance of this book is extended to the numerous Forest Service personnel and members of the environmental community who the author has interacted with over the course of over forty years. Forest Service personnel taught me over the years the culture of the agency; good and bad. In the sixties, these individuals gave me a valued glimpse into the agency created by its founding rangers. More recent personnel provided insight into the altered management of our forest from a single dominant use, timber extraction, to more balance and ecologically sustainable management. As deep an appreciation is extended to the numerous environmental activists I have known over the years. Most selflessly sought the betterment of forest management by the burdensome task of pouring through and understanding the many complex and technical documents produced to underpin a forest plan or a particular management action. The telling comments and suggestions they made turned the tide in the forest planning process. The most effective had walked the land and knew the land as well or often better than the federal managers. Activists like Richard Kuhl and Jim Connor of the Flathead region, exemplify the numerous activist whose concern for the forest lands was selfless and based on knowledge of the forest lands. These activists were unpaid and had nothing personal to gain, yet they carried the political battle that transformed the management of our national forest in the last twenty years.

I am indebted to the fine Roosevelt biographers; Brinkley, Goodwin, Millard and Morris. These authors' outstanding scholarship has provided insight into the great intellect, activist, and masterful politician that Theodore Roosevelt was.

Glen Truscott a now retired long time employee of the Forest Service who served in the trenches of the agency reviewed the manuscript and made critical comments. Hana Truscott translated my vision for the cover artwork into the fine tradition of a political cartoon. As with all my works, my wife, Donna Harvey was called upon and responded admirably to assure a readable text.

www.ingramcontent.com/pod-product-compliance
Lightning Source LLC
Chambersburg PA
CBHW070356290526
45790CB00004B/1520